*There is a bit of insanity in dancing
that does everybody a great deal of good.*

Edwin Denby

# DANCE LIFE

## ALSO BY THE AUTHOR:

### Wild Life: Travel Adventures of a Worldly Woman
Life Series #2

### Exotic Life: Travel Tales of an Adventurous Woman
Life Series #1

## CO-AUTHORED 1ST EDITIONS:

### Wild Writing Women: Stories of World Travel

### Self-Publishing Boot Camp Workbook

# DANCE LIFE

## MOVING' & GROOVIN' AROUND THE GLOBE

Lisa Alpine

true tales of an adventurous woman

LIFE SERIES #3

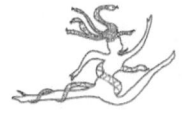

DANCING WORDS PRESS

*Dance Life: Movin' & Groovin' Around the Globe*
Copyright © Lisa Alpine, 2020
First published in the United States of America by
Dancing Words Press

All rights reserved. No part of this book shall be reproduced or transmitted in any form by any means, electronic or mechanical, including photocopying and recording, or by any information storage and retrieval system, except as may be expressly permitted by the publisher. The scanning, uploading and distribution of this book via the Internet or via other means without permission of the publisher is illegal and punishable by law. Please purchase only authorized electronic editions. Your support of the artist's rights is appreciated.

Requests for permission should be made via email to:
Dancing Words Press
www.LisaAlpine.com

I have tried to recreate events, locales and conversations from my memories of them. In order to maintain their anonymity in some instances I have changed the names of individuals and places, I may have changed some identifying characteristics and details such as physical properties, occupations and places of residence.

ISBN 978-0-9842293-8-3

Cover image: "Ballet: Vacate" by photographer Brooke Shaden
www.brookeshaden.com

Book and cover design: Scott Jordan and Lisa Alpine
www.TheScottJordanGroup.com

Typesetting: Typesetting India Private Limited

Printed in the United States of America
Copyright © 2020 Lisa Alpine, All rights reserved.

# GRATITUDE

*I want to be strong, I want to laugh along,
I want to belong to the living.
Alive, alive I want to get up and jive!
I want to wreck my stockings in some
jukebox dive.*

Joni Mitchell

From dancing on my mom's hip as a baby to reading the Persian poetry books and hearing stories of my dad's life in Turkey in the 1930s, I was infused with a love of whirling and of exotic places from infancy. Disneyland never interested me.

Paris did.

Palestine did.

Petra did.

I've been dancing, traveling, and spinning tales for five decades. Wrecking my stockings at the ecstatic dances in the jungles of Hawaii amid tattooed youth. Salsa-ing with gold-toothed men on the beach in Cuba. Second-lining in New Orleans' funeral parades. Mamboing with Mexicans in colonial plazas.

This is what Joni was talkin' about!

With deep gratitude I dedicate *Dance Life* to the creatives who have influenced me to be bigger and bolder in my exploratory forays into the realm of wandering, words, and movement—Joni Mitchell, Isadora Duncan, Rodin, Tim Cahill, Dervla Murphy, Gabrielle Roth, and so many more.

# CONTENTS

Introduction . . . . . . . . . . . . . . . . . . . . . . . . . . . . . . . . . . . . . . . 13

Rodin Woke Me Up . . . . . . . . . . . . . . . . . . . . . . . . . . . . . . . 17

The Stories: . . . . . . . . . . . . . . . . . . . . . . . . . . . . . . . . . . . . . . 21
from 2019 to childhood

Dancing With the Living . . . . . . . . . . . . . . . . . . . . . . . . . . . 23
Mexico 2018

Where God, Anchovies, & Flamenco Reside . . . . . . . . . . . 35
Spain 2018

To Trust or to Run: a woman traveling solo . . . . . . . . . . . 49
Morocco, Turkey, Mexico 1982 - 2017

Sugar Granny and Her Dancing Shoes. . . . . . . . . . . . . . . . 57
Cuba 2015

The Twerking Nun of Korçë . . . . . . . . . . . . . . . . . . . . . . . . . . . 77
Albania 2013

Queens of the Nile . . . . . . . . . . . . . . . . . . . . . . . . . . . . . . . . . 89
Egypt 1998

The Chilean Cliff Carver . . . . . . . . . . . . . . . . . . . . . . . . . . . 105
Ibiza, Spain 1993

Dusting the Dance Floor . . . . . . . . . . . . . . . . . . . . . . . . . . . 115
Ibiza, Spain 1993

Spiritual Grace Under a Blue Black Sky . . . . . . . . . . . . 125
Bali 1986

Two-Steppin' and Pussy-Poppin' . . . . . . . . . . . . . . . . . . . 131
New Orleans 1977-1982

The San Francisco Dance Lady . . . . . . . . . . . . . . . . . . . . 153
San Francisco 1974

The Garden of Eden . . . . . . . . . . . . . . . . . . . . . . . . . . . . . . 165
San Francisco 1974

How I Got Kicked Out of the Pecan Pie Club . . . . . . . . 173
Denmark 1972 & Oklahoma 1973

Olé in Paris . . . . . . . . . . . . . . . . . . . . . . . . . . . . . . . . . . . . . . 185
Paris 1972

The Flying Frug . . . . . . . . . . . . . . . . . . . . . . . . . . . . . . . . . . 199
California 1965

Dancing Diamonds ............................................. 207
California 1963

Dance Bites: ................................................... 211

An Invitation ................................................... 213

Tina Turner Still Has Legs ..................................... 217

Hands Dancing Freely ......................................... 219

Daylight Dancing ............................................... 221

Kalani Is My Dance Home ..................................... 225

Travel Shorts: .................................................. 227

Freedom From the Shadows .................................. 229
France 1972

Licking Ice Cream in Bolivia ................................... 233
1975

The Dancing Birds of Fez ..................................... 239
Morocco 2017

What Travel Has Taught Me .................................. 241

Epilogues: ...................................................... 243

The Beauty of Losing Our Fear ............................... 245

Elevate Us from the Shadows ................................. 247

About the Author: .................................. 249

Dancer, Heal Thyself .............................. 251

Kudos. ............................................. 255

# INTRODUCTION

*Strange travel suggestions are dancing lessons from God.*
Kurt Vonnegut Jr.

Perhaps the strangest travel suggestion I've ever received was an invitation to Albania to teach salsa at an orphanage—even though I'd never taught salsa. Ever. This peculiar journey birthed the story "The Twerking Nun of Korçë." Cha-chaing in a bikini at age 60 on a beach in Cuba with a hottie? Being kicked off a pecan farm in Oklahoma because I disco-danced with a dark-skinned man from the Congo? Having my heart pulled out in the flames of flamenco in a Spanish barrio while noshing on tapas? My love of dancing has always played a whimsical role in these surreal experiences that now grace the pages of *Dance Life: Movin' & Groovin' Around the Globe*. Some stories feature dance as a focal point, others are more about the travel experience, but movement is the glue.

*A writer is a world trapped in a person.*
Victor Hugo

Translating experience into words in this crazy, colorful world has always been my anchor. It adds meaning and sense to my wild wanderings as I weave words around a nugget that arises from passion and yearning. This ember, this word-hunt, holds me captive until the tapestry of the story is complete.

> *She decided to free herself, dance into the wind, create a new language. And birds fluttered around her, writing "yes" in the sky.*
> Monique Duval

Dancing is a dizzying place of joy and curiosity—what movement will come next? What feelings will swell up and overwhelm me, yet drive me home to my center? It's a free ride to galaxies of expression.

I especially love to dance under foreign constellations. Places speak to me most clearly when I am joyous and ecstatic.

> *Awaken your spirit to adventure*
> *Hold nothing back, learn to find ease in risk*
> *Soon you will be home in a new rhythm*
> *For your soul senses the world that awaits you.*
> John O'Donohue

Why am I a travel addict? I yearn to explore new worlds and interact with people different than myself.

Even as a toddler, curiosity about what was around the next corner led me down paths, under the house, crawling along fence lines. My mother in a panic—where did her tiny, frail girl go? Calling the police. Finding me in an empty lot fingering the soil, looking for bugs or at a stranger's house eating cookies. This wonderment has led me around the world for decades. I cannot help it—this desire to discover and uncover stories of people and place.

Dancing takes me inward; traveling takes me outward.

Writing maps the journey.

Turn these pages and swirl with me through Egypt, Bolivia, Albania, Bali, Cuba, Morocco, California, Oklahoma, New Mexico, Louisiana, Spain, Mexico, and France.

Enjoy!
Lisa Alpine

# RODIN WOKE ME UP

*The dancer of the future will be one whose body and soul have grown so harmoniously together that the natural language of that soul will have become the movement of the body. The dancer will not belong to a nation but to all humanity. She will not dance in the form of nymph, fairy, nor coquette, but in the form of woman in her greatest and purest expression. She will realize the mission of woman's body and the holiness of all its parts. She will dance the changing life of nature, showing how each part is transformed into the other.*
Isadora Duncan (1877 – 1927)

Freedom through dance. Freedom to be strong and daring, authentic and original. Isadora Duncan lived this throughout her entire *wild* 50 years on this planet. To this day, almost a century after her sudden death by scarf strangulation in a sports car on the Italian Riviera, her stories and dances continue to invoke the unfettered joy of free-form expression. She is the mother of modern dance.

Like Isadora, I was born in San Francisco and moved to Paris at the age of 18. And like her, I've explored the spontaneous territories of improvisational dance. Paris is where I first uncovered my desire to experience a place through dance interpretation.

It happened on a rainy winter day in the Musée Rodin. Rodin's monumental marble humans were so lithe, yet fully fleshed. Just appreciating the art form visually was not enough. I longed to get under their alabaster skin—to feel their exquisite shapes in *my* body. I craved the visceral connection to Rodin's hands as he chiseled these beauties into life. This desire emboldened me, and on that day in 1972, when I should have been attending art history classes at the Sorbonne, I stood in front of *Fugit Amor* at the Musée Rodin. Paralyzed by the couple's straining sensuality, and then enlivened, I found my body responding—turning *into* the shape and form of *Fugit Amor*. I reached deep into my being to embody their entwined muscular passion. Its beauty awoke a grace in me—a commitment to interact with art, architecture, nature and other beings, paying homage through movement. I continue to honor art through my body wherever I travel. A gnarled tree in Molokai, a cathedral's spire in Mexico, a pagan well's dark depth in France—these shapes enter my body and I'm allowed to physically experience the geomancy and magic of their spirit—for nothing is inanimate. Every detail and cell is fueled with energy and purpose to come together and make that particular shape. I co-create with the creator. Quite a nice way to interact and play.

Perhaps the tree roots catch my eye as I'm hiking in Molokai with my dance students. The worn, buff-hued ironwood root ridges snake above the ground, beckoning me to disrobe and wind my body next to them in waves. The earth is prickly against my flesh, yet I smell the tree's skin and feel its journey across the dirt.

Or is it the dozens of hanging winnowing baskets on display at the Institute of American Indian Arts in Santa Fe, New Mexico, that cause me to pause, yearning to get acquainted? Their disk shapes, suspended by filament from the ceiling, speak to me of circular movement. I start them spinning and then walk between them, repeating their turning motion with my limbs and spine. Our shadows dance on the walls, and I feel an ancient native presence in the room as I activate each basket. The curator is both horrified and fascinated as I move hypnotically among them.

What about those steel girders and metal rivets in a sculpture known formally as a bridge near Sierra Hot Springs? My students and I get out of the car in the middle of the bridge, which is suspended over a dry arroyo in the California high desert. "Let your dance be influenced by the shape of this structure" is all I give them as instruction. "It is all art, all the time." They climb onto the beams and bend into angular shapes, mirroring the geometric lines that cut across the turquoise sky, swallows darting about the dancers' heads.

In Paris I stroll under the bronze night sky after a reading at a Shakespeare & Co. celebration. Champagne, oysters, laughter. Gaiety follows me into the boulevards and parks of the City of Light. A gold-lit sculpture calls to me—spires rising from the grass like dragon fangs or Zeus's thunderbolts. Their sharp yet sensual edges lure me, a siren song inviting me to press my body into their shapes and flit between their golden teeth. I can't resist; they glow divinely. I *have* to experience them.

This obsession with translating art, nature, architecture into spontaneous dance interaction has a name. I call it "sculptural movement." I invite you to practice it and become intimate with your surroundings. You *are* the art form, in constant creation with all of life. Let yourself be moved; participate in your environment—children do it all the time!

Isadora and Rodin would applaud you.

# THE STORIES
from 2019 to childhood

# DANCING WITH THE LIVING

Mexico 2018

I went to San Miguel de Allende for *Día de Muertos* (Day of the Dead). But I didn't dance with the dead—no matter how many cemeteries I wandered through, gawking at gaudily decorated graves, during this macabre annual celebration.

As is custom, to entice the dead to journey back to the world of the living, bribes of their favorite food and beverage were laid out in tempting displays in front of every burial plot. Some gravestones dated back to the 1700s. Chicken mole and large bottles of tequila were by far the most popular gustatory offerings. I'd think the ancestors would get tired of chicken mole year after year, but there it sat, freshly prepared on dinner plates on countless graves, along with the intricate decorations family members had piled onto their relatives' tottering tombstones and crumbling crypts.

The altars of bright marigold petals and hot-pink chalk designs were flamboyant—not somber—but there were no funeral jigs or skeleton waltzes to join in. Instead, my travels during Día de Muertos found me dancing with very-much-alive, joyous Mexicans in settings as diverse as cantinas to parking lots to a torture museum café.

Side-splitting laugher accompanied me on this grand adventure, but first I had to get over my fears. I suffer from tourist phobia, which is hypocritical because I am one. Usually shunning popular destinations, I found myself inexplicably drawn to the expat haven of San Miguel de Allende in Mexico. Why had I avoided going to San Miguel all these years? Trepidation that I would be surrounded by mostly white, rich, faux-artsy Californians, and Texans who enjoy cheap maid service and dress like Frida Kahlo on Halloween. Cringe.

San Miguel's renowned writing community was the lure—I had signed up for a workshop on completing your book manuscript, thinking this would kick my book over the finish line. Alas, the workshop was canceled, but I was still eager to experience Mexico during Día de Muertos—one of the most colorful pagan traditions in the world. But the main reason I wanted to go was to speak Spanish. Latin languages are so poetic. Food for the communicator in me—for the artist in me. I find Spanish to be more romantic and lyrical than Teutonic English. I had learned it during my years as a South American importer decades earlier, and enjoy honing my skills by traveling to Spanish-speaking countries.

Gleefully convincing myself I would work unsupervised on my book during vacation, I succumbed to temptation and went on the trip anyway.

San Miguel stunned me in many ways. It's a World Heritage site, classically lovely with cobblestone streets and houses splashed in hues of ochre, persimmon, pomegranate, and sunburnt orange. Two thousand hewn-wood doors stud the colonial buildings within the historical center of town. Curious, I stood in front of quite a few of these handcrafted behemoths and waited for the doors to creak open, hoping to see what lay beyond. When a door did open, serendipitously, the view within inevitably revealed a lush, verdant courtyard graced with bubbling fountains and filled with twittering songbirds. The columned homes made of brick and tile surrounding the gardens could have been straight out of *Architectural Digest*.

This place was heaven for any aesthetic hound or culturally thirsty traveler. I did meet a few expats—five percent of the population are foreigners, but many of them stay within their luxury compounds recuperating from facelifts. Yes, Americans come here to get "work" done—just not the same kind that I was hoping to accomplish.

But to my surprise and utter delight, everywhere I wandered I was surrounded by teems of jovial Mexicans who swooped me up, including me in their festivities.

On my second day in San Miguel, I stood on the huarache-worn steps in front of the pink-stoned Gothic cathedral *La Parroquia*. Two other tourists and I bonded as we giggled at a bride wrestling with something in the back seat as she debarked from a vintage Rolls Royce limousine. It took her ten minutes to extract the troublesome satin-and-lace wedding veil and train. She pulled and yanked. She yanked and pulled. Two bridesmaids joined her and they tugged too. Finally, yards of material snaked out of the backseat to land in voluminous mounds on the cobblestones, looking like an albino anaconda. My new friends, sisters on holiday from Mexico City, and I laughed so hard we had to hold onto each other. The hilarity was contagious and soon their entire family was heehawing along with us.

After we'd caught our breath and wiped away the tears of mirth, they formally introduced themselves: Siblings Magdalena, Liliana, and Enrique; Liliana's two kids Erik, age 22 and Miguel, age 8; and Grandma Esther.

Magdalena pulled a silk flower wreath out of a shopping bag—the same floral halo all the other women in the family were wearing. She placed it on my head and said in Spanish, "Now we are sisters. Would you like to join us for dinner?"

Taken aback by their gift and impromptu invite, I hesitated and then said, *"Por qué no* (why not)?"

Winding down backstreets, we ducked into to a funky hole-in-the-wall cantina around the corner from the guesthouse where all six of them were sharing one room We indulged in Negro Modelos, mounds of piquant guacamole, and sombrero-sized platters of chicken mole enchiladas—a most popular dish for the dead and the living, apparently. Enrique got the party started when he flagged down a strolling mariachi band and negotiated a price per song. We danced and sang for an hour in the space between the dining tables. I had met my tribe: folks who dance uninhibitedly, sing at the top of their lungs, and hoot with laughter.

In between our sing-alongs to *"Bésame Mucho"* ("Kiss me a lot") and *"Guantanamera,"* they raised their frothy beer mugs in unison and said, "You must come with us to Guanajuato tomorrow for the Cervantino Festival."

"I'm supposed to go on a garden tour," I said. A sad puppy pout spread across the table. Even Miguel, the eight-year-old, looked bummed.

I shrugged, then, nodding wisely, said, "What is more important—new friends or a garden tour?"

This caused a riot of clapping and ordering of the mariachis to sing a boisterous rendition of "Cielito Lindo." Everyone, including Grandma Esther, jumped up, linked arms, and shouted the lyrics: *"Ay, ay, ay, ay, canta y no llores* (sing don't cry)." This was followed by enthusiastic hip gyrations from the sisters and Erik waving his hands wildly in the air like a tornado, knocking over a few waiters in the process. You'd think Mexico had just won the World Cup. How could I possibly have said no?

The next morning at 7 a.m., steaming coffee in hand and their wreath on my head, I met my newly adopted family back in front of La Parrochia. They were all dressed up—heels, makeup, fancy shirts, and shiny slacks. Next to them, I felt underdressed in my yoga pants, but at least I had chosen a royal-blue silk blouse and had gussied up with chandelier earrings and a cut-velvet scarf. And they admired my Skechers, which I had chosen because they doubled as dance shoes, as I had a sneaking suspicion dance would be part of this adventure.

I had no idea what the Cervantino Festival was or how far away Guanajuato was, and I didn't care. The fun began right when we piled into their van. First stop: the gas station—up went the music volume. Everyone except Grandma Esther tumbled out, dancing on the tarmac, to the surprise of the other customers. It was still only 7:30 in the morning—and they hadn't had coffee yet.

We danced and cavorted every place we stopped. They were on a road trip to forget about recent illness and loss. Within the last three months, Enrique's wife had died from an aneurysm and Grandma had survived a double mastectomy.

"Life is hard," Enrique said, tears edging around his eyes.

Frequently Liliana, Magdalena, or Grandma Esther would reach over and hold my hand.

"Thank you for trusting us," Liliana said.

I replied, "Thank you for trusting me. How do you know I'm not an axe murderer?" This made them pause and glance at me sideways, and then we all broke into gales of laughter.

Tragedy had a smiling face during the two days we spent together. Laughing and crying. Dancing and hugging. Joking and jostling. Sadness and joy. More crying. It was all there, shared openly with no burying of feelings.

We danced amid their tears at almost losing their mother. We macarena-ed through the ringing of Liliana's abusive boyfriend calling her every half hour. "Dump the bastard," I told her.

We danced through Enrique's suffering. He bought a little grey-and-white crocheted cat to place on his wife's Day of the Dead altar. "Maria Elena loved cats. She had five," Enrique shared with me.

They were fully in the moment and lived Ram Dass's creed *Be Here Now*, though I doubt they even knew who he was. And they included me, who had only just entered their stratosphere. They genuinely liked each other and hugged a lot, whether it was the pudgy 8-year-old, the gay 22-year-old, or the myopic granny. They included me in their flamboyant and frequent demonstrations of affection— hugging and giving me neck massages on the tour bus rides and when we shuffled down slippery mud stairs into silver mine shafts. And my dream had come true—they didn't speak an iota of English so I got to chirp in Spanish 24/7.

When we arrived in Guanajuato a few hours later, Magdalena asked me, "Where do you want to eat?" She was the purse holder and bean counter for their vacation funds.

Aware that money was tight for them, I said, "Wherever you choose."

They conferred among themselves. As cheap as possible was the verdict, so we joined the swarms of Mexican families crowding through the wrought iron doors into the central market. We shared a breakfast of shredded pork shoulder tacos and *bolillos* (buns) stuffed with beef, pickled hot peppers, and dripping with grilled onions.

I asked Grandma Esther, "How many people come over for Sunday dinner?"

"Forty-eight."

"How many?" I asked incredulously.

"Sometimes 65. We all live near each other."

"You must have a very large dining table!"

Esther grinned, her eyes twinkling through coke-bottle glasses. "I have 14 great grandchildren."

I playfully punched her in the arm and said, "You're four years younger than me. At 65 years old I'm so far behind you in the progeny department—only one son and zero grandkids."

Shaking her head, she said, "*Qué lástima* (what a pity)!"

I turned to Erik—Esther's grandson. He had nudged himself next to me and was plying me with chili peppers to test my stamina. After my sixth pepper, Erik said, "I thought gringos were hot sauce wimps."

Feeling emboldened by the chili peppers, I asked, "Does your family accept you being openly gay?"

"They don't mind. The only rule is I can't kiss my boyfriends in front of my little brother." Erik rolled his eyes, but this sounded reasonable to me no matter what sexual orientation he was.

"What music do you have on your iPhone?" he asked later when we were sipping Pepsi and eating spicy peanuts in the torture museum café (once a papal prison). Guanajuato has a plethora of gruesome, weird, and tacky museums. My adopted family wanted to visit them all *and* eat the horrid junk food sold at food stalls in front of the attractions, from gelatinous pig foot tacos to fluorescent taffy to "monk's balls"—a cloyingly sweet chocolate bonbon.

On a sugar high from the treats they were fattening me up with, I turned up the volume on my phone and Pharrell Williams' song "Happy" blasted from the small speaker. Erik squealed, "I love this song! and jumped up and grabbed my hand, and we did a lively salsa right there in the cafeteria. Soon the entire room was up and dancing—it had overtones of a Mexican daytime TV musical. Next up on the playlist was a Spanish version of Ed Sheeran's "Shape of You," which rocked the house. Even the workers were doing the windy-windy and lip-syncing behind the counter.

At sunset, djembe drummers playing extemporaneously at the vista point overlooking the shimmering lights of Guanajuato got us going again. Liliana started a conga line with Erik and me, who held onto her waist as she sped around the plaza. I looked behind me at one point and saw that our snake had grown to more than 50 Mexican students waving beer bottles and cheering us on while also trying to maintain their grasp on the frenzied person in front of them. The whipping snake was spearheaded by a very energized Liliana—one hot mama in her tight jeans and lacy tube top. The other dancers circled around us and started to bounce up and down with the drummers pounding out the beat with fury. I pulled a hamstring muscle showing off my high kick, but the pain didn't stop me—I just popped an ibuprofen and sashayed back into the mêlée.

The entire family spun and shook their booties gleefully as twilight faded. It was like a Mexican version of American Bandstand to wild jungle beats in the dark of the night. Just when I thought my feet were going to fall off, we piled back into the van. They had to return to Mexico City and work the next day.

Stuffed between flannel-shirt-clad Erik and his amiable aunt, Magdalena, I was warm and snug. Just before dozing off, I asked, "How long a drive is it to San Miguel?"

"Two hours," said Enrique, who was driving.

"Isn't Mexico City in the other direction?"

"Yes."

I sat straight up. "But it's late! I can hop on a bus from Guanajuato to San Miguel, no problem." Never mind that the word "hop" made my hamstring cry out at me.

"No way!" they yelled in unison. "We're taking you all the way."

As the cathedral bells clanged midnight, they dropped me off in front of La Parroquia with hugs and kisses and tears, and their trademark sad puppy expressions. Pulling myself away, I limped back to my lodgings.

The next day, still sporting the frayed flower wreath and missing all the hugs, I wandered into yet another ornate chapel to get a good look at the statue of Mother Mary. She was dressed in a baby-blue gown and peered down, glassy-eyed, from the altar. On my way out of the church a silver-haired man with a sparkling smile said, "Sit down. Join us." I hadn't realized that a small group of parishioners had assembled while I'd been gazing at the Virgin Mother. And join them I did—kneeling and praying to Mary out loud with my new buddies in the pews around me. I've never been religious and don't know the prayers, but the man next to me made a point of singing loudly into my ear so I could join in. I even crossed myself a few times, probably in the wrong direction. After an hour, they suddenly rose (my knees were grateful, particularly after the beating they'd taken the night before) and filed into the aisle.

A gentle hand guided me by the elbow into the center of the procession heading toward the altar. My friend the prayer coach and another man hoisted a saint's icon perched on a palanquin onto their shoulders and we proceeded to circle the church, chanting. I was a foot taller than the other processionaires and the only non-Mexican. It reminded me of a slow conga line danced to a dirge instead of marimbas. Many circumambulations later, I ducked out of the line and headed back into the sunshine, chuckling to myself that I seemed to be magnetically attracted to conga lines.

Later, as I walked across the Civic Plaza, I heard my name being called from the street. There was my prayer coach driving a pickup truck. I waved, then went over and asked, "Can I hop in and drive with you a short way?"

"*Por supuesto!*" He said with that same warm smile spreading across his face.

As we bumped along the cobblestones, I asked, "What was your group doing in the church? Was it a special novena for Day of the Dead?"

He laughed. "No, no. Our group of 12 people from my neighborhood meet every Monday and pray to Mother Mary. It is very powerful. You should join us. Afterward we meet at my house for dinner and music."

"I'm sorry, but I'm going back to the States in a few weeks," I said, feeling a tug of sadness.

This is how friendly Mexicans are—they tuck you under their wing and include you in their life.

I felt complete permission to be my exuberant dancing self in Mexico. I didn't have a moment to write—too busy dancing. Not one word made it onto the page, but I did wear out two pair of shoes and spoke a dictionary's worth of Spanish. The culture and language even permeated my dreams, which were colorful swirls of movement and laughter, all in Spanish with no subtitles.

Alas, the frivolity faded on the day I departed. A grey veil of dullness dropped over people's faces as soon as I landed in Houston. No smiles, no nods, no help figuring out immigration lines. No laughing. No hugging. Definitely no dancing! Just dreary annoyance written across everyone's face.

*Boy, if there is ever a time America needs to dance, it's now!* I thought as I looked at my fellow citizens.

To keep my spirits from deflating now that I'm back home, I watch the video of my Mexican family dancing in the cantina. Enrique's staccato laughter rings out in the background as he films Liliana, Magdalena, and me cavorting to the mariachi players. Erik and Grandma Esther send me Facebook messages daily; bunnies and balloons are Grandma's go-to emojis. The entire family insists I visit them next spring and I will take them up on their offer. I want to sit at Esther's humongous Sunday table with four generations of happy people. I want to do the cha-cha-chá around platters of chicken mole. I'll load my iPhone with more favorite dance tunes.

Between now and then, there will probably be more to mourn. Someone will have died, someone will be sick, others suffering through unknown tragedies. But the veils will lift, the spirits will visit, and we will dance.

# WHERE GOD, ANCHOVIES, & FLAMENCO RESIDE

Spain 2018

Flamenco was a fire I did not want to stick my hand into, yet there I sat in the front row at the club, just a foot away from the dancer poised on the stage. Her muscular back was turned to the audience, the floor-length ruby-red dress embroidered in roses clinging tightly to her, cinching in her narrow waist. With her black hair pulled into a sleek ponytail and an enormous silk chrysanthemum crowning her head like a Wimbledon hat, she was reminiscent of a super-feminine Frida Kahlo in flamenco garb.

Slowly, silently, she pivoted, raised her arm, and pointed an accusatory finger at the audience.

That jabbing finger said it all: *cheater, heartbreaker, unfaithful lout!*

*You! You! And you!*

I knew she wasn't pointing at me specifically (I'd never even seen her before, after all), but my instinct was to duck and cover from her scorching glare.

Far from finished, she lowered her arm. She was just warming up. A guitarist and singer joined her onstage.

Then came the decisive moment: she clawed at the hip-clinging skirt, pulled it up her thighs with lacquered fingernails—and began to dance. The guitarist's hands blurred in a strumming fury as the dancer's feet pounded out the beat. The singer's eyes bulged as he hit a high note.

I squirmed in my seat.

During intermission Jordan, my partner, leaned toward me, waggled an eyebrow, and asked, "Don't you want to take a lesson?"

That is the reason I came to Jerez—to study flamenco with a teacher who might consider taking on a visiting foreigner. The performances I'd seen in California were lovely, cultural events that included large portions of paella and pitchers of sangria. The Parisian cabaret where I'd been introduced to flamenco 45 years ago had been a hoot. No one had looked as if they wanted to stab me or stomp on my face with their heels. Theatrical—yes—but in a more romantic, friendly way.

The invitation came in an email from a man I'd never met. "Would you like to stay at my apartment in Jerez de la Frontera in Spain? Jerez is the cradle of flamenco and I've read your stories. Dance plays an important part in your travels and Jerez is undiscovered in this regard. Stay as long as you want."

And I did. For six weeks. Jordan came with me as he not only loves to travel, but to dance, too.

We arrived in May by train from Barcelona. *Atico*, as our sponsor called his getaway apartment, was perched on a rooftop patio in the old *barrio*. Atico means penthouse in Spanish. We were surprised when we turned the key and a cozy man-cave greeted us. Our host had a sense of humor, it seemed, for he had installed Wild-West-style swinging saloon doors that hit my behind and propelled me into the bathroom—before the morning coffee kicked in.

Out the windows swallows churned through the air, swooping over the tiled roofs and circling the myriad church steeples that punctuated the skyline. Bells clanged from all directions, announcing the time on the quarter-hour. There was no need for a watch in Jerez and also no need to travel far. Every site and activity was a short walk away from the Plaza del Arenal—a plaza so elegant it was fairytale book perfection, with parades of towering royal palms and a mirthful fountain featuring the requisite conqueror on a nostril-flaring horse rising from the spray.

The small river stones used to pave the promenade around the square were mosaicked in a wave pattern. As Jordan and I sat on our favorite bench we wondered how old the polished pebbles were. How many generations of well-dressed people of Jerez have clicked their heels on these stones?

We chose that bench not just for the view, but because it was the only place we could get a Wi-Fi signal. While the locals sauntered and nodded to each other, we were checking email. Flocks of little girls in miniature flamenco outfits and stubby-legged boys with red scarves tied around their waists stumbled and ran around their parents' legs. Grandfathers who passed holding hands with their cherubic grandchildren would *tsk* and shake their heads when they looked at us glued to our iPads.

After our daily communications, we'd follow the stream of families to a nearby ice cream store. As Jordan and I crowded around the glass case with all the children to drool over the vats of luscious creaminess, the owner leaned across the counter above the kids' heads. In a conspiratorial whisper, she said in Spanish, "I have a special flavor every day, which I keep in the back—it is not on display. Today is orange and cacao. It is my most favorite. You should try it."

The small scoop was black as tar and it crowned a homemade waffle cone. Back on our bench in the plaza, we licked—and our eyes popped in surprise. This was the yummiest bittersweet, tangy, candied ice cream *ever. Ever. Ever.* Its potent flavor reflected the intensity of the dark-eyed people of Jerez. I can see why the lady didn't want to serve it to the kiddies: this was adult ice cream. Sexy yet bitter—flamenco in a cone.

Almost everyone who swirled past us on the plaza was worthy of a good stare. Nattily dressed elderly couples strolled past us arm-in-arm—the men decked in tailored suits, pocket handkerchiefs, watch fobs, Borcalino hats set at jaunty angles; their matronly wives in calf-length dresses and patent leather handbags. The younger women were mannequin-perfect with smooth complexions, their flamenco dresses emphasizing curves. Yes, full on flamenco regalia: lace-edged skirts trailed on the stones, florid fake flowers topped their heads, and giant loop earrings skimmed their shoulders. These getups would look garish on women of any other heritage but here, as they fluttered around us on the plaza—getting on buses, standing on street corners, shopping at the Mercado Central—the effect was superlatively peacock. Jordan and I were like guppies in our Target attire. Puzzled, we wondered, had we landed in a 24/7 flamenco costume party or maybe a Carlos Saura movie set? Didn't anybody in Jerez wear regular clothes?

After we finished our ice cream, we went into a flamenco dress emporium to see what these ensembles cost. Maybe I would get one, even though I knew I'd probably look ridiculous.

"What's with all the polka dots?" Jordan asked.

"No kidding," I said. "I thought the only women who could rock polka dots were Audrey Hepburn and Marilyn Monroe."

Hundreds of ruffled, floor-length dresses in every bright color and pattern (screaming roses, zigzag stripes, *and* giant polka dots) hung limply on racks. Without women filling them out, pressing against the diagonally cut seams, these garments were tacky and lifeless. I'd seen dresses make a plain woman gorgeous in, say, Paris, but never witnessed a woman make a gaudy dress shout *Olé!* I left empty-handed. These flamenco outfits were pricy—between $300 and $1,000 apiece—and would never fit in my wheelie bag.

The next day, during our daily gawking session on the bench, an old man in a fedora sat down beside us. "You are not going to the Feria del Caballo?" he asked in Spanish. *"La feria más importante de España.* Women, dancing, tapas, lights. And the horses! They are *Pura Raza Español,* a breed whose ancestors have lived here for thousands of years. You must go. There is nothing to do in town. Everything is closed during the feria. Even the banks. And the fair is free."

"*Qué es una Feria del Caballo?*" I asked, looking at him quizzically. "*Vamos!*" he exclaimed as he grabbed my hand and motioned for Jordan to get off the bench. He led us to a bus stop teeming with costumed fair-goers.

As we bumped out of town in the standing-room-only public bus, our tour guide explained that the horse fair is held annually at the fairgrounds, where the entire population of Jerez descends for a week to promenade, eat tapas, admire the famous Andalusian horses bred and trained locally, and dance the Sevillana.

After fifteen minutes, the bus stopped and everyone poured out toward the ornate fairground gates. Our new friend tipped his hat and said, "Don't just sit like birds on a wire; try dancing the Sevillana. Sevillanas are danced by couples of all ages and sexes during celebrations, often by whole families and towns. It is very graceful—not like the ferocious flamenco danced in the clubs. It is the elegant spirit of Spain."

Families and businesses sponsor cafes, or *casitas*, where a dance floor is laid down, tapas are served, the patron pours drinks, and people pack in from noon to midnight for those seven days. Normally, the casitas at the feria are closed to outsiders, but in Jerez you can shove into the crowd and mingle—dancing to salsa, reggae, rap, reggaeton, or joining a group Sevillana. The music style depends on the generation that sponsors the casita.

Everyone was dressed to the nines. Darting this way and that, throngs of women blurred into Technicolor schools of tropical fish, using their fans for exclamation-point-like rudders. The men strutted behind their shoal in tight toreador-style jackets, broad-brimmed felt hats, and highly polished boots with a slight heel used to make a masculine stomp when doing the Sevillana.

We were anthropologists studying a culture preserved in amber. Even many of the modern women wore the exact mode of dress and adornment that their mothers, grandmothers, and great-grandmothers had donned. Fringed shawls concealed their cleavage and bodices, and thick eyeliner and six-inch heels punctuated all this finery. Shiny, coal-black hair in ropy curls snaked around their shoulders. Some of the younger women had elaborate tattoos on their backs of flowers, vines, jungle birds, and butterflies, revealed by their low-cut dresses.

Women danced with women, children danced with their grandparents, flirtatious couples roistered around each other. And all around them, spectacular Andalusian horses circled the fairgrounds, pulling ancient carriages piled high with bouquets of women who waved and snapped their fans at friends and hooted at paramours.

The feria lured us back every day and late into the evening. Did we rise up off our seats and dance the Sevillana? No, but we did edge into the smiling crowds and salsa when salsa was being played.

When the feria ended, the locals Cinderella-ed back to everyday apparel, their multitude of costumes packed away until next May when the Feria Del Caballo would take over Jerez yet again.

The tabancos reopened, and we now had a new world to immerse ourselves in—flamenco shows.

Until I arrived in Jerez, I had never heard the word *tabanco*, so I asked the owner of the café downstairs from Atico what it was.

He set down a café manchado (coffee stained with milk) and told me that they were small neighborhood venues that sold tabacco, tapas, and drinks. They also were a place singers, dancers, and musicians could congregate and jam. Many were gypsies living in the barrios. Not too long ago, he went on, the streets were empty and the tabancos had to shut due to a recession, but recently there had been a resurgence of interest in them from the younger generation, who wanted a place to socialize and celebrate their heritage. So now, every afternoon and evening the streets of Jerez teemed with crowds drinking beer, sherry, or wine, and eating tapas. It was an affordable way to mingle.

Every block in our barrio had a tabanco, and many offered flamenco shows during the afternoon and evening. Locals also brought their guitars. Someone rapped a beat on the tabletop, guitars were liberated from their cases, and everyone joined in the ballad. No one was texting or calling. No one was taking a selfie. Everyone was actively involved in the cacophony of music and boisterous conversation punctuated by animated hand gestures.

The intimate twelve-tables-plus-a-bar Tabanco Cruz Vieja on Calle Ramón was our favorite, and just a few doors down from Atico. For an eight-euro cover charge we experienced a larger-than-life immersion into the passions of roiling guitar strings, syncopated clapping, flurrying skirts, and stomping heels. How the small wooden stage held up under their fury, I had no idea. Every show was different and each performance topped the one before it.

On our regular Sunday afternoon visit, we were at our usual table right in front of the stage—almost *on* the stage. Seated next to us was a man with a palm-sized, cross-eyed furball of a dog who was not fazed in the slightest by the noise. It was too busy scarfing paper-thin *jamón serrano* slices his owner dropped surreptitiously under the table. This pet *really* liked its tapas and yipped whenever the supply dwindled.

The man gave us a once-over. "I don't see Americans here very often. May I buy you a drink?" We talked about Jerez and flamenco. Something pulled at my pant leg and the man tossed the pooch an anchovy to keep it quiet before saying, "These people have an unfair advantage over us foreigners." He was from Belgium and his daughter was studying dressage at the Royal Andalusian School of Equestrian Art in Jerez. "Look at the babies in the strollers. When they hear flamenco, their feet kick to the beat of the music—before they can even walk. How can we expect to learn this at our advanced age? The pregnant mothers keep time on their bellies, so their babies come into the world with rhythm."

The waiter, a handsome fellow with a lock of hair draped over one eye, managed to set down armloads of tapas on the postage-stamp-sized table for us to nosh—shrimp fritters, Mediterranean anchovies, triangles of aged cheese, pork cheeks in sherry sauce, and grilled peppers. I could hear excited snuffling from under the table, but I was not going to give any of these delicacies to the little beggar.

A glass of sherry appeared. *"Buena medicina,"* the waiter said, and nodded his head at the caramel-colored liquid.

As soon as he left, I turned up my nose. "I don't like sherry; it reminds me of cough syrup. My grandmother drank sherry."

Jordan said, "Sherry is a fine drink if you're a well-behaved woman. And you're sitting in a parlor."

I gave him a look. *Wise ass.* "Which I am not."

But to be polite, I took a tiny taste—and instantly changed my tune. It was dry yet creamy, with hints of cinnamon and almonds. Jerez is the Spanish word for sherry and *bodegas* (cellars) are all over town. The aging sherry barrels seep vanilla-oaky scents that hang over Jerez in an aromatic cloud. This glass of palo cortado sherry was the perfect pairing with tapas.

The Belgian saw the expression of delight as I took my second sip. He told us that *palo cortado* means "cut stick," in reference to the mark made on the cask when this style of wine is being made. Palo cortados are derived from finos or amontillados, which are marked with a single line. When, during the wine-making process, the vintner determines that the fino or amontillado is instead becoming a palo cortado, he draws a cross—or a cut—through the initial stroke—or stick.

This guy knew his sherry!

I loved our olive-eyed waiter. From that moment on during our twice- or thrice-weekly pilgrimages to Cruz Vieja, he would ceremonially place a palo cortado in front of me, along with the savory tapas du jour. All this was included in the cover charge. And he always said with a wink, *"Buena medicina!"* before he dashed off to serve other customers.

The dog settled itself under the legs of the Belgian for a nap, and just as a seared, salted pepper slid down my throat, the performers entered—a guitarist, a singer, and the dancer.

## Where God, Anchovies, & Flamenco Reside

The guitarist thrummed and the singer wailed. The dancer turned stiffly toward us, smacked her palms together, and eyed us skeptically. As she threw her head back, the music accelerated and her footwork took off, skimming the stage pockmarked from a history of percussive heels. The dancer's spine curved into an indignant arc. She was excruciatingly beautiful.

Incredulous, I gulped down an oily anchovy. The flamenco dancer raged and twisted, storming across the stage to the vocal howling of the singer, whose neck veins swelled as he squeezed painful notes from his throat. His face turned pomegranate.

Still terrified by the dancer's fiery glare, I chanced a look around me. The Belgian was right about kids absorbing the music by osmosis: a gypsy girl stood in the aisle next to us, snapping her fingers and holding her arms overhead, imitating her mother onstage. Her brother sat nearby on a banquette, tapping on a soda can to the pulse of the guitar.

As the blistering guitar notes subsided, the singer stopped and looked down at his feet. The dancer unfurled her fists, dropped her skirt hem, and turned to smile upward toward heaven where God, anchovies, and flamenco reside. Her kids clapped and hooted their applause even louder than we did.

It was fortunate Atico was nearby, as the performance had exhausted us. We needed a nap.

On another night, the featured tabanco performance was a memorably robust male dancer, tall and fair, in a tan business suit and seriously sexy snakeskin boots. When he came out on the stage, he loomed over our table.

The giant flamenco dancer leapt with both feet into the air like an angry toddler. He crashed down, snapped his fingers, and shouted, "*Olé!*" Then, in a tornado of passion he performed a high kick, just missing knocking Jordan's hat off.

"Subtle is obviously not part of his repertoire," Jordan hissed, ducking down.

The dancer landed on the stage with a deafening stomp and another triumphant "*Olé!*" He was Bruce Lee and Nureyev combined. Our jaws hung open at this man's athleticism and spitfire footwork.

*Why couldn't we just sit in the back?* I wondered. It felt like we were in the middle of a karate film. The dancer thrashed his arms up and down, flipped his sweaty curls out of his eyes, and stared fiercely at us while jackhammering with his feet. His stage name could have been Raging Bull. Alarmed, I watched the plate of pork cheeks slide across our table. Our glasses rattled. The dancer was on a tear. We couldn't avoid him as our table edge was one inch from the stage.

A placard with my name on it had reserved this intimate *and* intimidating seating. After the first show or two like this, we tried to sit at the bar, which was a good 30 feet away from the stage, but before my derrière had landed on the bar stool, the proprietor came at me like a freight train, grabbed my elbow, plucked the placard from behind the cash register, and firmly escorted us to our VIP position in the front. There was no escape.

I had no idea why he considered us important and worthy of display. The waiter descended with piles of food and drinks we hadn't ordered but voraciously consumed. Flamenco gave us an appetite—even though we were just observers.

Over the course of several weeks, we became acquainted with Theigo Vazquez, the organizer and guitarist for most of the shows at Cruz Vieja. He must have had connections with every great performer in Spain, because the lineups were always stellar.

At intermission one night, I sat next to Theigo at the bar. I had some burning questions to ask him about flamenco. He seemed quite calm and relaxed, a sharp contrast to his stage persona.

"Are you a gypsy?" I asked. I'd always fantasized about being a gypsy.

He smiled gently at me. It was a beautiful smile. "Of course," he said. "Flamenco is in my blood, on my father's side. My mother is Brazilian."

"Ah, that's where your *saudade* eyes come from." In Portuguese, *saudade* means a mix of sadness and paradoxical joy derived from acceptance of fate. I found myself staring longingly into those soulful, obsidian eyes framed by luxurious lashes.

As he gazed back at me kindly, I felt emboldened. "I have another question for you. What does *olé* mean?"

Theigo reflected on the question as he fiddled with a cigarette lighter and said, "I can't completely explain this magical moment when we give ourselves to the music and share this feeling together. *Olé* is when you feel that connection. *Olé* is a call of recognition from the soul."

"Why is the style so painful? So sorrowful?"

"Flamenco is like your American blues. You have B.B. King; we have El Caracol. Even the lighter *alegrías* are sad—yet you are crying with happiness."

Suddenly, I sensed a restlessness behind us. We both turned. The dancer was pacing the stage. Theigo put down his beer with a bow, picked up his guitar, and joined his tribe.

As I returned to my seat, Jordan waggled those bushy Groucho Marx eyebrows at me again and asked tauntingly, "So, what about that lesson?"

As the guitar strings growled to life before me, I contemplated the realities of learning flamenco. I had witnessed the intricacies and steps at the club and realized my improvisational way of absorbing and integrating new dance forms was not going to work with this highly technical form of dance. I shuddered to think of what would happen if I tried busting a move at the inappropriate moment during a stern class, and frankly, I'm just not pissed off enough to dance flamenco. Shouting and stomping are not part of my personality.

So this time, I had an answer for him. "These dancers have daggers for eyes. I'm more of a sixties flower child."

For once in my life I felt it was okay to sit and watch and clap. To cry out an *"Olé"* along with everyone else. To sip palo cortados as these masters of dance commanded our attention, their heads thrown back in timeless defiance.

# TO TRUST OR TO RUN: A WOMAN TRAVELING SOLO

### Morocco, Turkey, Mexico 1982 - 2017

"Fez's streets are narrower than a slot canyon," says Tim Cahill.

They aren't quite streets, yet they lead to people's homes. Many people. Behind these carved, crooked wooden doors are a multitude of families dug deep in the warren of plastered rooms behind thick walls that weep moisture. Fez sits on an aquifer and is not as bone-dry as the shades of dusty adobe suggest.

Tim is right—the streets are a mysterious maze of twisting dark passageways no wider than a donkey's back. I get lost every time I wander out from my *riad* (traditional Moroccan guesthouse). Really lost. For hours. This is the magic of exploring the oldest and largest medina in the world—an intriguing, disorienting experience, especially for a Western woman wandering alone who also likes to experience the local music scene and go solo to dance clubs at night, which can expose me to dicey situations.

I'm in Fez for a storytelling workshop and Tim, an intrepid explorer and renowned travel writer, is the instructor. I arrived five days ago to decompress and get a feel for Fez on my own.

"I'm afraid of the dark alleyways," the other female travelers in the writing workshop say when they hear about my solo explorations of Fez. "How do you walk down these shadowy, twisting backstreets without the safety of numbers or the protection of a male companion?"

*When to trust and when to run?*

As I ponder this pivotal question that arises frequently during my journeys, I answer, "Trust your gut. If your gut is sending you warning signals, run like hell unless you're a ninja black belt. There are times when you can't be a polite, nice girl. You have to get out of there, and pronto! At that point who cares if your instincts are wrong—it's not worth sticking around to find out. And don't hesitate. Just do it."

I still chuckle when I remember one instance when I ran like a whipped racehorse—not caring what my handsome, sensitive musician escort thought of my hasty flight from the unlit Malecón of Puerto Vallarta, Mexico. I had met him in a hotel restaurant where he was playing flamenco guitar and he invited me for a walk after his performance. He seemed gentle and interesting, so I wrapped a shawl around my shoulders and we strolled out into the starry night. The waves were crashing on the beach and our conversation was easy. It was late and no other people were on the boardwalk. As we continued it seemed more and more deserted—until I saw a man up ahead peering at us from behind a wall. Stories of tourist muggings intruded into my thoughts as I looked over at my new friend. He was very delicate in a pretty way. The shape of the man ahead of us ducked back into the shadows again.

Red alerts were now flashing in my gut. Without a thought—or a comment to my oblivious companion—I turned heel and ran. All the way back to my lodgings. That poor guitarist was abandoned with no idea as to why I disappeared, but after so many years of traveling alone, when I get afraid and I'm in a situation that feels unsafe, I respond. Instantly. Perhaps the shadow man was not interested in us at all. Maybe he was out smoking a cigarette or going for a stroll himself. But what if he was a mugger, or worse? Puerto Vallarta is not the safest place to wander in the dark.

I remember another time where there was absolutely no question.

Three years ago in Istanbul, I was in a taxi heading to the airport for my return flight to San Francisco. The driver grinned crookedly at me through broken, stained teeth. The smile torqued into a leer. His direct, rheumy stare was distressing and I squirmed, not wanting to look at him. We were on the boulevard, skirting the ramparts. His hand was in his lap and when the subtle rubbing motion started and then amplified, so did my discomfort. Was he fingering his prayer beads or something less sacred? It quickly became apparent that it was not prayer beads he was stroking but the sausage-shape rising under his shiny, tight rayon pants.

*Get out of the car now!* my brain screamed. Could I sit here, captive to this perversion one more minute?

Was I willing to miss my flight?

*Get out now!* shouted every cell in my contracting body. I looked out the window; if I could just make it to the sidewalk,

I could easily hail another taxi on this busy thoroughfare. Slamming my fist into the seat I yelled, "Stop the car!"

His hand lifted from his thin, stained pants, and his beady, mean eyes drilled into me from the rearview mirror. In a raspy, angry voice, he yelled back in Turkish. I didn't need a translator; he was not a nice man.

I leaned forward and screamed in his ear, "Stop!"

Reluctantly, he pulled to the side of the road on a narrow shoulder. I pushed the door open as the rush hour cars sped by. He glared at me in the rearview mirror, bellowing and rubbing his fingers and thumb together in the universal sign for money.

I didn't give a fuck.

But my suitcase was in the trunk. Spittle flew over his chin and onto the windshield. Turkish is an ugly language when spewed by a grizzled pervert.

*Suitcase suitcase suitcase.* Should I sacrifice my suitcase and jump to the curb, praying he'd drive off?

Fear morphed into fury. *I'm not giving him anything!* One foot stayed in the taxi and I shouted and pointed to the trunk.

Then, a distant form of a man appeared, walking toward us along the sidewalk on the other side of the road.

"*Monsieur, monsieur,*" I yelled, trying to keep my foot anchored in the taxi while waving and calling to the man.

He started to run. He was young, tall, good-looking, and as he got closer smooth, hip music emanated from the ear buds under his cap of curly black hair. His handsome face was concerned. In English he asked, "Miss, what is wrong?"

The driver is touching his penis. I'm going to the airport to fly home. I do not want to be in this horrid man's car, but my suitcase is in the trunk."

The young man sprinted toward the driver and let him have it in furious Turkish. The driver shoved the rusted door open, shouted back at him, and pointed at me as if I were the devil's consort. The vile man then opened the trunk, threw my bag on the ground, and screeched away, tires spinning.

The kindly man stood protectively close to me and hailed another cab, sternly telling the driver to get me to the airport without any shenanigans. He turned his lovely, chiseled face toward me and said, "I'm so sorry. Please know he is the old Turkey. But remember me—the younger generation—who respects women. You are beautiful and I hope you have a safe voyage home." He opened the taxi door, took my hand, and kissed it in a tender, respectful manner.

I made my flight. My hand bore the sweet imprint of his kiss, yet my body reeked of the adrenaline activated to get me out of that hellish taxi.

*When to trust and when to run?*

My story stirs up a lot of discussion among the other writers in the workshop, most of whom are women emphatically nodding their heads in agreement. I point out that men usually don't believe these stories of harassment—they think I have a chip on my shoulder or I'm imagining the seriousness of danger present—and the women nod some more. But one woman sits forward and says, "You are stereotyping Turkish men! Why did you even get in that taxi?" One of the younger men adds, "I think you're exaggerating."

We all turn and look in disbelief at the man.

Tim is enjoying the heated dialogue and says, "This is what a good story does—it stirs up the pot. It makes you think." Then he points out, "The taxi driver was obviously a dick."

Tension is defused as we laugh at his reference, and he asks me, "So, what about here in Fez?"

I explain that here in Fez I have had no issues. The medina is not riddled with dark, foreboding alleyways, but threaded with thoroughfares that lead to neighborhoods and homes. If I did feel endangered by a man coming from behind, then I would lift one of the weighty brass knockers nailed to every door and I would bang it loudly. When the door was heaved open and a headscarved woman stared from it at me in alarm, I would explain in jittery, childlike French that I was scared and that I'd rather be safe than sorry. In Fez, it's more than likely that when I look over my shoulder again at the man coming closer, I'll see that he is carrying a plastic sack of blossoming cilantro, scarlet tomatoes, rotund onions, and a plucked chicken. In all probability, he is not a threat—just a neighbor bringing home the ingredients his wife requested for dinner.

That afternoon, I push open the *riad*'s large, heavy door and enter the winding route that leads me deep into the medina. A curving alley thick with dancing dust motes beckons, and my feet turn down the narrow cobblestone lane.

A man's raspy laugh disrupts the stillness. A frisson of alarm ripples across my skin. Then a child's laughter responds, intertwining with the man's voice and relaxing the grip of fear. Savory roast lamb and tantalizing, smoky eggplant waft from a nearby window, twisting around my nostrils—an invitation to continue down this well-lived passageway.

*When to trust and when to run?*

I have asked myself the same question when I go to dance venues—many times solo. Recently, while in Paris, I went out nightly to fabulous World Music clubs. Sometimes they were located in sketchy neighborhoods. I'd take the metro into outlaying *banlieues* (suburbs) to hear famous groups from Senegal, Cuba, Algeria, Brazil, Armenia, Ghana, Bolivia. Music is food for me and dancing is a crucial ingredient in the satisfying feast of listening to live bands from distant cultures. But while immersing myself in the experience, I'm also aware of my surroundings. My radar is turned on. Are men dancing too close with insinuating glances or can I let go and abandon my body to dance bliss? It can be a tightrope as dancing is a sensual sport. And can be misinterpreted.

Then the question becomes: when to dance and when to depart?

# SUGAR GRANNY AND HER DANCING SHOES

Cuba 2015

I love to dance and have always dreamt of living in a culture where dance is the national pastime. When I decided to travel to Cuba in November 2015, I was thrilled to find in my research that Cuba was pretty much the closest thing I'd find to that definition.

Everyone I'd met who had traveled there raved about the salsa dancing in clubs, on the street, in classes, on rooftops, even in elementary schools. Didn't matter where these travelers went, Cubans danced around the clock. A big motivation to visit for a dance addict like myself. And pronto—before the hordes of Americans who were expected to arrive within the year, spewing from humongous cruise ships. I wanted to get there before the Cubans toned down their dance vivacity to a Disneylandish blandness.

How to pack for a country that had been—until recently—off-limits to most American travelers? Due to Fidel Castro's

Communist intolerance of religion, covering my hair and body was not an issue as it was in most of the countries I'd visited. On the contrary, Cubans appeared to delight in strutting their stuff. YouTube videos showed local dancers in clubs and pedestrians along the Malecón wearing mismatched clothing with flip-flops, tennis shoes, or tottering high heels. Faded fabrics pulled tight across pendulous breasts, wide derrieres stuffed into flesh-toned stretch pants, and the worst—short-shorts with low-hanging butt cheeks—were the fashion of the day. The economic hardship and famine of the 1990s that Fidel Castro called the "Special Period in Time of Peace" were definitely over. Cubans were no longer rail-thin and there was nightlife and tourism to supplement their poverty-level income. So packing was simple: bathing suit, hat, cotton pants, two dresses, and a jacket. No short-shorts or hot pants.

Travel blogs and guidebooks recommended bringing pens and bars of soap as gifts—items Cubans needed that were in short supply due to the embargo. That seemed mundane, cheap, and slightly offensive. But how about earrings? Earrings are lightweight, and who doesn't like sparkly jewels? Guys could give them to their girlfriends, wives, or daughters, and I could wear them until I gifted them all away by the end of the trip.

The conundrum was shoes. My challenge was to travel light with only one pair, over cobblestone streets, up muddy mountain trails, and—most important—dancing till dawn.

It was a tough hunt for the ideal all-purpose footwear. I hate to shop. But at last, on the day before departure, I found them. Black Skechers with an insole, tread, and soft soles that would pivot smoothly on the dance floor.

I was ready to dance—bopping to a hot mambo, changing partners in a fast-paced square-dance-style *rueda*, and dipping into a sultry bolero. I was sure that by the end of my trip, my shoes would be falling apart after endless hours of dancing.

All my travel accoutrements were packed and weighed less than 18 pounds—the maximum Air Cubana allowed for carry-ons. I planned to travel for one month from north to south—the full 800-mile length of the island. The backpack-suitcase and perfect shoes were just the right stuff for chasing down a departing bus or taxi with ease.

After the seven-hour flight, Havana's outline appeared through the taxi window. The air blowing into the rattling taxi was scalding hot, the sun blazing white. Horses grazed on the meridian. The tall, tropical palms lining the boulevard morphed into buildings with collapsing roofs, and a cacophony of bicycle taxi bells filled the air around me as I entered the heart of the city.

Havana at last. Smoggy Havana. Noisy Havana. Falling-down Havana.

Settling into my lodging in the rundown yet picturesque port area of Old Havana, I asked Mildred, the proprietor of my guesthouse, *"Dónde puedo ir a bailar?"* Where can I go dancing?

Mildred was a schoolteacher, and her favorite music was punk rock. "You can go to a club in Vedado. It opens at midnight. Bring earplugs. I would go with you but I work tomorrow."

*How the heck do you salsa to punk?* I wondered.

Instead, I slipped on the new black shoes, dipped into my earring collection, and headed to the Casa de la Música de Miramar—a place my friends had raved about. "I saw Los Van Van there" or "I heard Eliades Ochoa from Buena Vista Social Club," they'd exclaim. I, too, was hoping for a big-name band and hot *salseros* (salsa dancers).

Impatient to get my dance on, I went to the afternoon show at the Casa de la Música de Miramar. A tight group of young men gathered around the entrance. I pushed past them to pay my $10 and enter the club, where darkness and the stench of stale alcohol greeted me. Purple neon above the bar provided the only light from which I could see tables crowding the dance floor, but only a few were occupied. As my vision adjusted, I noted several Cuban women in tight dresses and stilettos sitting solo at the scattered tables. No music played, no band was on the stage. Just women looking like they were waiting for customers.

"When will the music start?" I asked the waiter.

"*Tal vez en dos horas*," he said.

Two hours was too long to stay in this depressing place, so I returned to Mildred's to read a book on my first night in Havana. My shoes sat by the bed like forlorn puppies.

Later, Mildred confessed she didn't have the money for the club entrance and that most Cubans don't go for this reason. She makes $17 a month teaching fifth-graders—that's the standard salary for everyone from doctors to bus drivers. The $10 entry fee I so eagerly paid, plus the two-drink minimum pushing expensive, water-downed mojitos made with sugary soda instead of fresh lime and cane juice was more than most locals could afford. No wonder there were only *jineteros* and *jineteras* (male and female hustlers) and tourists at the touted Casa de la Música.

From my ongoing inquiries to strangers on the street over the next few days, I discovered that younger Cubans don't even like salsa music.

*"Por qué quieres bailar a eso?"* they'd ask. Why do you want to dance to that?

I'd say, "I thought Cubans love salsa music."

"Are you kidding? That's for old-timers," they'd reply, their noses turned up in disdain. "We dance to reggaeton and rap."

Well, this was a rude awakening! Were my friends who had been to Cuba hallucinating, or did they not realize they'd been led to tourist traps? I went to bed wondering what style of music reggaeton might be, suspecting it was a derivative of Jamaican reggae dancehall, which is tediously repetitive and overtly sexual.

Refreshed from a quiet night in my room, I hit the cobblestones early the next morning searching for the perfect *café tinto*, culture, and—oh, please—salsa dancing.

I'm very attracted to pagan spiritual practices, which usually include music, or at least drumming. Hence, I gravitated to the Museo de los Orishas in Havana, a museum I had heard about in a voodoo shop in New Orleans several years ago, dedicated to the Santería religion and their pantheon of gods or orishas. Santería is a syncretic afro-Caribbean belief based on magic that goes back to ancient African Yoruba roots, wherein orishas are emissaries of God almighty, ruling over the forces of nature and the endeavors of humanity. This tradition spread from Africa along the slave-trading routes and is practiced in the Caribbean, Brazil, New Orleans, and Cuba.

On the way to the museum, I discovered an open-air hardware market selling oil lamps made from tuna fish cans, antique irons, and coffee pots you put directly onto the flame. Among one vendor's trays of rusted keys and cookware, rolls of wire and lighters, and neon posters of saints, were piles of brightly-colored beaded bracelets. I like jewelry and headed over there like a fish seduced by a shiny lure.

An ebony-skinned woman leaned against the display, smoking a cheroot. She motioned me forward and, in a husky, hushed voice, mysteriously asked, "Which orisha is yours?"

Surprised, I said, "Yemayá." Yemayá is the goddess of the sea, of whom I became enamored in Salvador da Bahia in Brazil 40 years ago. In Brazil, they practice Candomblé, which means "dance in honor of the gods" and has the same origins and deities as Santería.

Her eyes lit up. She nodded in silent recognition and held up her wrist. The woman was wearing sea-blue beaded bracelets that identified Yemayá as her spirit guide also. She slid a similar chunky azure-blue bracelet onto my left wrist.

"Put it on your left for protection," she intoned several times, looking me steadily in the eyes and not letting go of my arm. "Not the right," she reiterated.

I asked my perennial question: "Where can I go dancing?" The vendor's eyes lit up again. "Come to my house this Sunday for the birthday of my other orisha—Orunmila—the god of wisdom, knowledge, and divination. There will be lots of dancing and drumming. My son can pick you up and drive out to the countryside where we live."

I was confused about these multiple gods and asked, "What do you mean by your 'other' orisha?"

"You have your primary god who protects you and then a second—sort of like a *padrino*, or godparent. You must honor them both. Who do you think your second one is?" she asked.

I closed my eyes, instantly transported in my mind to a place of sparkling waters and dazzling white clothing swirling around me. "It must be Oshún—the goddess of rivers and streams," I replied. "She came to me in dreams when I was in Brazil." Both Oshún and Yemayá are worshiped in Salvador da Bahia.

I spent a month there during Carnival in the 1970s and danced into the ocean and a river mouth with the Candomblé priestesses. They would wade up to their waists in the gentle surf, soaking their hoop-skirted white dresses. On their heads were baskets of flowers and fruits that they would place on the surface of the water as offerings to the goddesses. The blossoms and fruits floated out with the tides as the crowd danced and chanted, hypnotized, behind them, and I never forgot the connection I felt with those women or with Oshún and Yemayá.

"Ah—I can see her in your body movement," the vendor said, bringing me back. "The way your hands dance when you speak. Fluid. She is Yemayá's little sister. Oshún's color is yellow."

The woman dug through her mountain of baubles and lifted up a ropey, sun-yellow beaded bracelet that she wound around my left wrist above the blue one.

From the moment I wandered outside the tarp-covered market and into the harsh noon light, people nodded toward my wrist and made comments as they passed. "Yemayá?" I had been suddenly included in their secret spiritual society. It didn't matter that I was pale-skinned and a tourist. Over the next week, I noticed that many of the people who mentioned my bangles were wearing flowing white cotton outfits and turbans. Most of them had very dark skin, indicating they were from the east, near Santiago de Cuba—the hub of the Santería religion. Later, I discovered that the all-white garb I'd been seeing in these poorer parts of towns was for Santería initiates who wear it for a year and practice the religion's guidelines of purity.

The docent in the orisha museum was, similarly, very interested in my bracelets and asked, "How long have you been initiated? Which orisha is your second? Did you do the year in white?" I was beginning to feel like a poser, even though the friendliness and camaraderie continued when I couldn't answer her questions.

Later, I walked back through La Habana Vieja (Old Havana) into other districts, looking for souvenirs. One of the main shopping streets was packed with food vendors' carts and cheesy, doughy "peso pizza" offered from tiny windows cut from home kitchen walls. Women paraded past, showing lots of flesh in what appeared to be secondhand clothing—torn and ill-fitting, either too tight or too saggy.

Department stores were nonexistent along the crowded street, but there were a few dingy state-run stores with recycled clothing stacked to the ceilings. Most of the clothing is purchased in bulk from American Goodwill and Salvation Army organizations and shipped in containers to Cuba and other parts of the world (Albania has these same stalls).

Back on the street, no treasures in hand, nose itchy from the moldy piles of clothing, my head swiveled when a woman strode by me. Yes, she was wearing my rare, hand-painted Burning Man T-shirt—the one I had given away several years ago at the Salvation Army collection truck parked in front of a Safeway in Mill Valley, California.

That Sunday I didn't feel comfortable going to the party in the countryside, but I heard about a public party in the El Centro district in an alley painted with murals by resident artist and sculptor Salvador González that sounded promising, with live musicians and dancing in the streets. A well-known Cuban guidebook-writer-friend of mine had just been mugged here the month before and warned me about thieving and dangers in this part of town, but I ignored him and shuffled into the shabby neighborhood, hoping to get down with the locals.

As I walked down evermore dilapidated streets, the air hazy with pollution, I was amazed to find that the edifices were stunning in their faded grandeur. Like Elizabeth Taylor's or Bette Davis's face after years of drinking—puffy and blotchy but still glamorous in a ruined way. El Centro looked like I imagined a war zone would—a bombed, crumbling mess watched over by hundred-year-old carved angels and Doric columns.

It was a muggy, hot afternoon, and a large crowd spilled out from the Callejón de Hamel alley, where the dance party was being held. Amid the dozens of tourists pointing cameras were drummers and pickpockets bumping into people with furtive glances and nimble fingers. Souvenir stands with plastic saints and ashtrays were jumbled together in doorways.

Despondent, I wandered down potholed streets. Aside from the more publicized-than-expected dance party, El Centro seemed deserted, but I talked to a man on his stoop wearing a wife-beater and boxers. He was missing an arm. "Angola" was all he said when I asked him what happened. Then he told me he'd been part of the Cuban revolutionary army brigade that went to Angola in Africa and fought for the leftist People's Movement. The scar was a jaggedly done sew-job.

I wondered whether to turn left or right—or did it matter? Would I end up back in my room reading for another evening? Then, the sound of drumming arose in the distance.

I headed in the direction of the beat, which emanated from an open doorway in a private home. It was one of many small houses painted in faded pastel colors, crowded together along the empty street. All the doorways were open due to the heat and seemed deserted, but this one was a beehive of lively percussion. I leaned in. Before I could back away, thin arms pulled me into a crowded living room, and a chanting mass surrounded me—people reaching out to touch my bracelets. They were also wearing colorful beads around their wrists.

A dark, statuesque woman in a skin-tight red dress and towering yellow patent leather heels drew me further into the mayhem. A thick scar traveled from her chin to her mouth. A machete stroke to silence her, I wondered?

She beamed a gold-toothed smile and made space for me in the smoky parlor where young men danced beside middle-aged women wearing the ubiquitous hooker-style outfit—skimpy shorts and tops displaying super-sized thighs and bulging breasts. It appeared to be a pulsing room filled with tranced-out, dolled-up transvestites. Pressed into the corner were five drummers banging away in a sweaty frenzy, and a priest, who was leading the chanting and channeling Babaloo—the god of healing and strength.

The beat intensified. Dancers raised arms in the air and turned in circles until their eyes rolled back. I tried to keep up with the hip rotations and salsa-gone-dervish, which was quite a workout in the steamy, windowless room. It reminded me of being in the Amazon in the heat of summer with a high humidity factor. But I was so happy. Finally, dancing with abandon—with real Cubans! No gigolos or pickpockets.

The red-dress woman hooked her arm around my gyrating hips and led me down a narrow, paint-chipped hall into a room no larger than a pantry. Inside was an altar to an orisha clothed in yellow, and I touched the bracelet of the same-hued beads that the vendor had given me. Was this Oshún? The thought brought an even stronger sense of closeness to this group of dancers. Offerings of food, fruit, money—even toy trucks—were piled high across the floor and up the walls, surrounding a two-foot-tall doll in the corner. It looked like a Christmas present Uncle Stanley gave me when I was six years old—except this doll was chocolate-brown, not ivory-white.

A turbaned priestess lit votives arranged around the doll. The priestess was adorned in a frilly yellow dress that took up half the room and was a life-sized version of the one the doll was wearing. The woman turned to me and said, "Enter. You may say a prayer." I squeezed in, pushed a plate of cookies aside, and knelt on the cement floor beside her. She handed me a long seedpod rattle and guided me to shake it wildly in the air toward the bulgy-eyed plastic doll in the yellow dress.

The priestess gently clasped my arm, pulled me toward her, and whispered in my ear, "You may pray out loud or internally. Who are you praying to help?"

"My mother?" I said tentatively. (Even though my mother had died four years ago.)

"*Tu madre.*" The priestess nodded knowingly.

I closed my eyes and shook the rattle noisily above my head, praying for the well-being of my mother in the afterlife or wherever she was.

"*Tu madre está bien. Ella es feliz.*" As she patted my back, the warm-palmed priestess assured me my mother was well and happy.

I kissed the ground and slipped a couple Cuban pesos into the offering basket after touching it to my forehead as instructed. I stood, bowed, and backed out of the tiny room.

In the parlor I joined the dancers in more enthusiastic rhumbaing and singing. I don't usually sing in public, but I was fairly certain no one could hear me. The loud din of the percussion bounced off the walls of the boxy room that throbbed with 20 gyrating dancers.

The red-dress woman was back at my side. She encouraged me to shout and chant and groan, all while doing a funky-chicken-style salsa. She hypnotically whispered the words of the chants into my ear, then indicated with a ripple of her long fingers that if I felt goosebumps or chills I should dance harder and faster—so I did.

My guide's eyes were rolling back. She swayed like a palm tree in a hurricane, holding onto me for support. It was quite cozy. I felt included and needed, and I danced protectively around her, afraid she might fall and hurt herself, and me.

The woman returned from her trance and whispered, "Everyone in this room is suffering. From death, lost love, ill health. The ceremony is the only place we have for solace and protection." Her eyes rolled back again but then came back into focus as she stared hard at me. "We all have problems—everyone is here because life is hard. We all suffer." She told me, "Shake it loose. Dance it out. Let it go. Give it to the orishas. Unload your suffering. We are all in the same *manera* (way)."

My humanness made me one of them. I, too, had suffered. It had been very hard for me when my mother died, and I still missed her with a hole in my heart that couldn't fully heal. The bracelets were my membership card, and my shoes were really getting a workout. *This is better than salsa dancing*, I thought, letting the aching grief pour over me and then wash away, for a time, on the drumbeat. *It's spiritual*.

When I returned to Mildred's, I realized the bracelets were not simply adornments and reluctantly took them off. They matched my outfits and I liked making connections with these darker-skinned people practicing a religion from the distant Yoruba tribe in Nigeria. Drumming, dancing, and trance are my world—at home in California, I go to ecstatic dances weekly. But I haven't taken vows or practiced purity ceremonies and rituals. Where at first these bracelets had made me feel part of something, now they made me feel like an imposter. They went into a side pocket in my luggage, a memento of this ritualistic society that embraced and prayed for me even though I was an outsider from a rich, spiritually devoid country.

After this wild trance-dance in a postage-stamp-sized living room, I didn't dance again until I was in Santiago de Cuba two weeks later—in a shadowy courtyard crowded with garbage cans.

As I savored a late afternoon *café cortado* and creamy flan on the plaza in Santiago, an apricot-flamed sky lit up with bolts of lightning hurtled out of towering clouds. Surrounded by the dramatic thunder booms of the coming storm, I strolled through back streets. As the first drops of rain pattered onto the sidewalk, I ducked into the doorway of a once-grand apartment building where, blocking the entry, was a small table topped with a bottle of clear liquid and a folded towel. I had seen this in front of many houses and businesses in this city and thought that since Santiago is the epicenter of the Santería religion, it must be an offering to the orishas.

A skinny porter in a too-short uniform invited me inside. He gestured toward the altar and asked, "Did you wash your hands?"

"No" I said, mystified.

"Please wash your hands with the chlorine before entering. There is a cholera epidemic and eighteen people have died in the last two days."

Still not understanding what he meant, as no one had mentioned it before, I squeaked, "Epidemic? This is not an offering to the gods?"

He laughed and then nodded solemnly. "No, not an offering but a health precaution. You do not know what it is because the government does not want foreigners to know there is an epidemic, as it scares off tourism."

*Jeez!* I'd been a regular hugging ambassador in the streets of Santiago, wanting to spread American goodwill—clueless about exposure to a deadly disease. *Why didn't the guesthouse owner or taxi driver tell me when I arrived?* I quickly brushed away the question, deciding not to worry but to be on alert for symptoms. The chorine, though watered down, was harsh as

I poured it over my hands, and my nostrils flared and burned from the fumes.

Music was coming from far back in the building. *"Donde está la musica?"* I asked. With a crooked finger, he motioned me to follow him. We walked down a long, damp hallway lit by one bare bulb, which led to a grimy, covered courtyard lined with overflowing garbage cans, and the porter took a seat next to one. Apparently it was a slow day. In the center stood five men playing music—two conga drummers, a gourd shaker, a cymbal player, and a man who turned the handle of an ornately carved wooden organ from another era. The man was old and arthritic, yet he cranked the organ's handle with vigor as the music spilled forth.

The ancient organ player gestured for me to come over and look inside a large wooden travel trunk filled with stacks of faded songbooks—perforated cardboard sheet music that created the melody as he turned the organ's handle. Swooping calligraphy on the side of the instrument proclaimed it to be *"Le Orgue de Paris."* It was a treat to see such a relic from the past being played, not just on display in a museum somewhere.

The music was lovely and rhythmic, and I couldn't resist the urge to move. This was my first dance to authentic, classic Cuban music since arriving on the island three weeks ago.

One of the conga players rose, leaving the other to carry the beat on his own, and joined me for a smooth salsa dance and then a cha-cha-chá, despite the space restrictions of the tiny courtyard and the unpleasant smells wafting from the trash cans. He led me through the steps with ease and a gentle yet commanding hand on my waist—I held my own, thankful that my father had taught me these same classic Latin dance steps years ago in our living room. After several more tunes, the band took a break and invited me to sit with them.

I asked why they were playing in this claustrophobic courtyard, and they replied in Spanish, "We are professors of music at the university but have nowhere to practice. Our friend is the caretaker of this building and the acoustics are good. So here we are."

*Wow.* I guess acoustics win out over the stench of rotting garbage.

"You must come to hear us again and dance. We practice every Thursday." The octogenarian organ player stood, bowed, and planted a sweet kiss on my cheek. As I walked back to the street, escorted by the porter, I heard them say, *"Americana! Es una buena persona de una buena familia."* I smiled.

That night, I decided to give the Casa de la Música in Santiago a chance. It had the reputation of being home to great musicians. I quickly found, though, that it was the same sad story—hustlers pushing drinks and fat German ladies dancing with young Cuban men in an attempt at salsa that included a lot of butt-cupping. I found it interesting there was no hand-washing table in the front of the club's entrance, and felt fortunate to have discovered the music professors that afternoon.

By my last day in Cuba, I had given up hope of salsa dancing to a renowned band in a club. My shoes had gotten a lot more hiking experience than dancing in Baracoa—the southernmost town in Cuba and the first place Columbus landed. The town is situated on a postcard-perfect bay rimmed by tumbling green mountains and several national parks that can only be visited with hired guides.

Ricardo, a botanist guide recommended by my guesthouse owner, led me up steep, root-bound trails to mountain peaks with spectacular views. At another national park, we forded a turbulent, swirling river and hiked through cacao forests in dense jungle.

After four days of exploring the parks, we had become friends and I was teaching him English. Ricardo wanted to show me around Baracoa on his day off. "What do you want to do?" he asked.

"I want to swim in a river and swim in the sea." I didn't even bother mentioning dancing.

We did both, eating grilled red snapper and drinking passionfruit mojitos at a table in the sand. Diving into the clear, warm Caribbean waters. No tourists in sight. It was heaven. Then the music started up on a boom box. I tapped my fingers on the chair arms to the beat. A young man near me, a friend of Ricardo's, was swaying and smiling. At me. He slowly rose from his beach chair, walked over, and offered me his hand. The international invitation to dance.

Not only did this kid have rhythm—he was fun. He was both a perfect salsa partner and spontaneous. And like me, he just wanted to dance. And dance. And dance. Both of us could not sit down.

I was barefoot, in my swimsuit, ecstatically dancing on a Caribbean shore—not caring one ounce if my thighs were marbled and my neck wrinkled. My dance shoes sat askew in the sand, not needed for this dance-a-thon under the rustling palms.

When I got hot I'd dive into the sea and float on my back, staring up at the cloudless, turquoise sky. My dance partner paced back and forth on the shore, eyeing me and waiting for another dance. We went on like this until sunset. Four glorious hours of dancing.

It was time to head back to the guesthouse. Early the next morning, I was flying to Havana and then on to San Francisco. Still basking in this perfect day, I was saying goodbye and thank-you to my dance partner, the chef, and the locals who had gathered to watch the *gringa* dance on the beach, when my Casanova grabbed my waist and pulled me toward him. Breathing hotly in my ear, he crooned, "I will take you dancing to a *muy fantastico* club tonight."

The invitation was laced with other crap like, "You dance like a Cuban woman" and *"Mi amor,* your body is *muy fina."*

*Okay, that's enough. I'm three times his age!* Maybe he was partially blind? No, he was a horndog Cuban male hoping for a visa to the promised land. Then he tried to grope my ass.

*Drat!* He'd just spoiled my dancing queen beach day, but the sun was setting anyway, so it was time for Cinderella to head home and pack. I didn't realize Casanova knew where I was staying—and was a persistent young lad.

That night after my suitcase was neatly packed and I was in bed, pebbles pinged off the windowpanes of my room and a piercing whistle rose from the street below, waking me up. Pulling the curtain aside, I peeked out and saw my barely-legal ass-grabber. I ducked under the windowsill and doused the lights. The pebbles and whistles continued but finally died off after 15 minutes. I crawled back into bed and started to giggle in the dark, thinking, *OMG! I could have been his sugar granny!*

I almost fell out of bed, laughing till I cried.

Me—not a cougar, but a sugar granny. A lost opportunity for slithering, sweaty slow-dancing and heat-seeking hands against walls. Dark club lighting can be very forgiving.

The next day, back in the Havana guesthouse, I asked Mildred if she wanted to trade shoes. I'd heard Cubans really needed shoes and I'd already given away all my earrings. Her brow furrowed and then, as realization of my offer dawned, a huge smile bloomed across her face.

You'd think I'd offered her a pair of diamond earrings. She kissed me on both cheeks and hugged me tightly, squirming out of her flip-flops and sliding into my Skechers. She probably wore them to the punk club that weekend, hopefully paying the entrance fee with the extra $20 I'd slipped into the shoes before handing them to her. Her flip-flops fit me perfectly.

# THE TWERKING NUN OF KORÇË

### Albania 2013

It started off as a joke. A shared desire to go somewhere really mysterious and off-the-beaten-track with zero tourists—particularly Americans. Sitting in front of a crackling fire in Northern California, a glass of blood-red cabernet warming in our palms, we opened a *National Geographic Atlas of the World* in front of us. Dreamy-eyed, my partner Jordan and I turned the pages, traveling viscerally over the precarious mountain passes of Afghanistan, riding ponies across the Mongolian steppe, dragging our feet along the tundra, sailing a clipper ship to a sandspit in the Spice Islands.

Then, our fingers traced down the coast of Croatia, rippling around the stony islands clinging to the coastline of Montenegro, and bumped into Albania, perched above Greece on the Ionian Sea. It was a country whose borders I had skirted in 1972 while hitchhiking from Denmark to Greece. I remember that the young British man who had given me a ride in his Morgan Roadster along the length of the then-Yugoslavian coast shuddered when I mentioned that on the map, it looked like it would be a shorter route to Greece if we went through Albania. "No way," he'd said. "That country is a poverty-stricken hellhole. Plus, we'd be jailed for even trying to enter."

Jordan and I looked at each other. "Do you know anyone who's been to Albania?"

"No. Do you?"

"No."

"Let's go!" We swigged our wine like pirates plotting a raid.

We quickly found there was a reason travelers didn't go to Albania. It wasn't on the radar. Or, as my British ride accentuated back in 1972, it was not just forbidden but dangerous. For 45 years, until 1991, the country was cut off from the outside world. First by Enver Hoxha, a paranoid dictator who didn't let foreigners in or Albanians out. Then, by his successor, Ramiz Alia, the leader of the Communist Party. During this period, Albania was the most isolated and poorest country in Europe.

Not only is Albania off the radar for tourists, most people don't know where it is. Even my travel-writer friends. Jordan and I chuckled how it got a rise out of them when we said—with a straight face—"We're going to Albania. In two months."

They would tilt their heads and look at us skeptically. "Where is that? Why Albania?" they'd ask.

"Because you don't know where it is!" we would answer smugly, then we would laugh and laugh. Slap our thighs, wink at each other. Be obnoxiously elitist. In our minds, it was still a game we were playing that we'd actually go.

But the desire to explore somewhere untouched by Western civilization still dug into us. One morning, I read an obscure report from a German hiking club about the newly named Balkans Peace Trail—a meandering sheepherder and trader route that straddles the mountains between Albania, Kosovo, and Montenegro. It was the first time in a thousand years these borders were open. The hiking club's vague description made it sound like it might even be marked with trail signs and that the Albanian Alps were deliciously unspoiled—like the Swiss Alps before the onslaught of the jet-set crowd. I didn't know there *were* Alps in Albania. This country was becoming more enticing.

Suddenly it wasn't a joke. Without much ado, we booked cheap flights on Lufthansa to Istanbul and then Turkish Airlines to Tirana, the capital of Albania. Done!

On a whim, I posted our upcoming adventure on Facebook and asked if anyone had travel tips or connections.

Expecting radio silence after the response from our traveling friends, I was surprised to get a note from a former writing student. She remembered that 20 years ago one of the members of her church went to volunteer at an orphanage in Albania and stayed there after meeting an irresistible missionary. Would I be interested in connecting with her? After my emphatic yes, my former student got in touch with her friend, and two days later I received an email from the missionary, whose name was Beth. She queried: "Would you like to come to Korçë and teach our kids to salsa dance?"

Where she got the salsa idea is a mystery. Perhaps she had visited my website and read that I teach dance, but the page clearly states that my expertise is in creative/modern/therapeutic. There's not a word on there about salsa…

Still, who could resist such a wacky invitation?

Jordan and I salsa dance frequently—it was the glue that had sealed our union on the first date. So we knew what we were doing in some sense, but could we teach it? And would it be difficult to give dance step instructions in the Albanian language? Save the Children images paraded through my head. Perplexed, I contemplated the reality of teaching weak, malnourished orphans an energetic dance like salsa. We'd heard horror stories of recent conditions in orphanages in other autocratic dictatorships from Romania to Bulgaria.

On top of all this, our research had warned us about the perils of travel in Albania: gigantic ankle-twisting potholes, finger-busting gangsters, nothing to eat but 27 types of meatballs, no hot water, insane drivers, no English spoken.

But with the lure of hiking the Alps and giving dance instructions in the south, we threw our concerns to the wind and rhumbaed our way to the airport for our thirty-day adventure.

Our first night, we stayed at a youth hostel in Tirana and met our one and only American during the entire trip: a grizzly, disillusioned 80-year-old who complained he wasn't going back to the United States until a black man was *not* our president. We avoided him like the vipers we were told to watch out for on the mountain trails.

Albania turned everything written about it on its ear. We encountered no thugs, no meatballs, and found plenty of hot water, safe drivers, and English spoken. Sure, there were a few potholes. And poisonous snakes, of which we'd seen four, including the deadly Ursini's viper.

We hiked a portion of the Peace Trail, swam in the Ionian Sea, explored every UNESCO heritage site, discovered hot springs and ancient Ottoman bridges, drank stunning wines, and ate more food than we should have.

After three weeks, we circled around to Korçë in the southeast near the Greek border for our salsa gig. We settled into a dingy hotel, saw a gypsy with a dancing bear in the open market, and ate a yummy barbequed lamb lunch under a grape arbor. Then, dance shoes and iPod tucked into my purse, we wandered the narrow streets searching for the church that housed the orphanage.

The white plaster edifice topped with a bell tower took up the entire block. Its polished wooden doors were two stories tall and embedded with a giant brass knocker. *Bang, bang, bang.*

A short-haired, middle-aged woman dressed in jeans and a T-shirt pulled the door open. She was not the pale, stooped nun in a black habit and wimple I'd envisioned.

"Hi, I'm Beth," she said in an American accent.

She shook our hands, turned, and briskly led us down a well-scrubbed tile corridor to a large meeting hall filled with 45 teenagers and a half-dozen Filipina nuns who lived in the convent at the nearby cathedral and ran the orphanage there. The building we entered turned out to not be an orphanage but an evangelical church safe house for abused girls and gypsy street kids, a day care center, a school, an elder care facility, *and* a youth activity center—all organized by our hosts.

I was expecting peasant garb and poverty, like something out of a Dickens novel, but the teens were good-looking and well-groomed, dressed in jeans and designer shirts. With eager smiles, they lined up like in a Zumba fitness class.

"No, no, no," we said. "Come closer, circle around, and follow our feet." We used lots of hand gestures to illustrate, as our Albanian was still at the please-and-thank-you stage. When I held up my iPod with a questioning look, a young man named Bujar plugged the device into an elaborate sound system on the stage.

Bright, bold Cuban salsa music burst into the hall and just like that, the kids were wiggling enthusiastically. I'd assumed they'd be shy, traditional, religious, needing pointers on how to move their hips and keep a beat. Oh no. They were already popping and grinding.

Jordan took the boys to one side and I circled up the girls. Since we didn't really have a clue about the exact steps we were supposed to be teaching, we improvised, demonstrating our somewhat idiosyncratic version of salsa. Big smiles spread like sunshine across our faces. It seemed to be contagious: the teens happily partnered up and boogied around the floor with gusto.

Well-lubricated hips are a must for Cuban music, and getting those hips rotating was my job. Despite Jordan feeling miffed that I wasn't following his lead, I suggested the girls do their own thing and not follow the guys. I know that's not salsa but, hey, I'm from San Francisco and the era of freeform dancing in Golden Gate Park.

Surprisingly, the nuns were on my side. They tittered and clapped their approval as I demonstrated the windy-windy—a sensuous figure-eight hip sway I learned on a bar top one New Year's Eve in Honduras.

The big-boned European and American missionaries and tiny Filipina nuns hovering on the sidelines joined in. The nuns were really getting down, shedding their grey cardigans and shaking their hips. Then I saw something I never would have imagined. First, one of the younger nuns looked over at me and winked. Then, she slid her tweed skirt to right above her knees, slowly bent over, and twerked. It wasn't an over-the-top Miley Cyrus gyration; it was a modest rendition, to be sure, but twerk she did.

The kids burst out laughing and suddenly, the playlist of Latin beats on the iPod and the twerking nun had launched an unexpected party.

What struck me most was that, unlike many Americans, these teens were unselfconscious and weren't intimidated when asked to dance with new girls or boys—or even the nuns. Folk dancing is part of their home and social life, and as a result, they weren't awkward or picky about who they danced with.

Two hours flew by in a frenzy of fancy footwork and lots of laughter, and all too soon the school bell rang, signaling the kids to go to algebra class. Bujar, the sound guy, copied my playlist onto his iPod so they could continue salsa dancing—or whatever Albanian hybrid it had morphed into during our short lesson with them.

The last teen reluctantly shuffled out. Our appetites stimulated by all the physical activity, Jordan and I invited Beth the missionary and her handsome husband Christopher to dinner, thinking they probably didn't have the budget to dine out and could use a good meal. We, too, were up for a hearty repast because the next several days would consist of a long, bumpy, convoluted journey in Soviet-era busses across the Korab mountain range to Tirana and our flight home.

We asked them to choose the restaurant. Christopher pulled up in front of lavishly carved brass doors, which two men in well-cut Italian suits opened with a flourish as a valet parked Christopher's jeep. Perfectly polished Mercedes' and Humvees idled in line behind us. Christopher was greeted warmly with handshakes and invited with sweeping gestures to bring his entourage inside. Behind his back, Jordan and I raised a quick eyebrow over this seemingly well-connected missionary.

The foyer was decorated in hip Parisian-Moroccan palace-style. The maître d' escorted us through fountained courtyards to a quiet table, where chill European lounge music and groovy pastel lighting set the tone. The waiter, who looked like Johnny Depp, handed Christopher a 12-page wine list with a bow.

Glancing around, we quickly realized we were the oldest people in the crowd. Where were we? This restaurant had unveiled an affluent Albania we'd not seen in our travels thus far.

"Where did all this wealth come from?" I asked Beth under my breath as Christopher ordered a pricey bottle of wine. She saw the look of concern in our eyes and assured us, "Don't worry. They won't charge us for the wine. Christopher is revered in this town. Just two years ago, the mayor and the town council voted unanimously to make him an 'Honored Citizen of Korçë.'"

"What has he done to receive this honor?" Jordan asked.

Christopher's face went red as a beet. "Let's not talk about me," he pleaded softly, shaking his head.

Beth's eyes teared up as she told us his story anyway. "When he arrived in Korçë in 1991, right after the fall of the Communist dictator Alia, there was so much need—everything from distributing food to rescuing abused children. Christopher built all these social services from the ground up over the last twenty years and is now the Director of the Evangelical Church of Korçë."

Still pondering this glitzy oasis in contrast to the horrors Beth just related, I asked, "But where does the money come from that built this rich neighborhood with designer stores and fancy restaurants?"

Beth took a quick look around before answering in a whisper, "Albanian gangsters living in Europe send money home to their families."

This outpost of European swank housed several specialty bars and a disco, and served impeccable seafood and meats. I scanned the menu. Still no meatballs…

We spent half of our entire travel budget on dinner that night, but Christopher and Beth's stories were worth it. Originally harkening from England, Christopher had been a missionary in Bulgaria and, now, Albania for a combined 40 years.

In between bites of carpaccio, walnut-stuffed figs, forest mushroom ragout, lamb and eggplant, crispy green-pepper salad, and a dozen other delicacies, we leaned forward to hear their shocking stories.

"Have you ever lived through a period of anarchy?" Christopher asked us in a conspiratorial tone, putting his fork down.

"Just a few violent coups, riots, and curfews in South America," I responded.

"After Albania started getting back on its feet and opened its doors to the outside world in 1991, things went well for awhile. Then our economy collapsed in 1997 because of greedy pyramid schemes that sucked the life savings from hundreds of thousands of Albanians. A civil war broke out.

All day and night we'd hear gunfire; it was complete anarchy. We had to protect the orphanage. Those little Filipina nuns you met back there were brave and staunch—they guarded the front doors holding Kalashnikovs. The guns were the same size as the nuns but those women were determined not to let the marauders near the children, afraid they'd kidnap or harm their young wards."

"Where did the nuns get the AK-47's?" I asked, trying to picture the grinning, twerking nun I'd met just hours ago hefting an assault rifle.

Christopher leaned forward and let out a heavy sigh. "Every police station and military outpost was abandoned. Citizens needed protection. They looted the gun lockers, munitions, and army depots, desperate to fight off the gangsters flooding in from the south. Every kid over the age of ten had at least one gun, and so did our nuns."

After the waiter had refilled our wine glasses, Christopher continued, "This went on for over a year. Remember the photos of Albanians storming the docks and climbing up the anchor chains of Italian ferries and fishing vessels, trying to escape?"

I shook my head, recalling those images I'd indeed seen in the *Los Angeles Times* of thousands of desperate people scurrying over one another like ants, up the steel hulls and anchor chains of boats.

Christopher continued, "Now we're in a peaceful time of prosperity and it's thanks to remittances flowing in from Albanian refugees and gangsters in Europe and America. Two point seven million Albanians live here and three times that number are outside the country."

The stories continued to pour forth—as did the expensive wine—till past midnight.

Jordan and I never would have imagined three months before, when we were tracing our fingers along the then-unfamiliar Balkan coastline, that our spontaneous desire for adventure would lead us to this remote edge of Albania. Who knew that we would witness a twerking nun, teach well-dressed orphans to dance, and eat in a gangster-funded glam restaurant?

Who knew that we would salsa and sup with heroic missionaries—saintly rock stars beloved by the community for protecting the children of their city through dangerous times? Now these missionaries welcome foreigners to teach their children, opening doors that were once closed, and bringing culture—and extemporaneous salsa—to Korçë.

# QUEENS OF THE NILE

Egypt 1998

The night Stanley proposed to give me one million dollars to have a baby, I was sweaty and happy. Not from the offer of such an outrageous sum but because I had just danced with abandon to a heavenly song in a heavenly place.

Our Nile cruise boat was moored in front of the 3,300-year-old temples of Abu Simbel on the edge of Lake Nasser in southern Egypt. My traveling companions—five gay men, informally dubbed the Queens of the Nile—were in the discotheque. It was late. Most guests had gone to bed tired from their travels, including my mother, who was part of this flamboyant posse. I sat on a red velvet banquette on the edge of the dance floor, sandwiched between Stanley and my fellow dance partners: Miguel, a bubbly Latino who could salsa like a Cuban master; Richard, an old friend of Stanley's who had a rapier wit; Franco, who lacked personality but looked like a gent from GQ; and Ian, a mercurial opera singer whom Stanley was putting through college.

As I slid back onto the bench after another fabulously Arthur-Murray-esque contemporary waltz with Ian, my favorite dance partner, Stanley—the elder and initiator of this group of traveling queens—adjusted his cravat, leaned over, and whispered, "You and Ian are the perfect people to have a baby together. I'll give you one million dollars and I can be the godfather."

I guffawed, and then, knowing Stanley, stopped short. "My god, you're serious!"

Stanley stared me down with his piercing, no-nonsense gaze. He had the eyes of a sharp-shinned hawk. "I need an heir. You two are the ideal combination of brains, beauty, and grace."

"Stanley, Ian is gay. And 18 years old."

I felt like I was scolding a child trapped in the body of a 78-year-old mega-rich eccentric businessman, whose assets included an Asian seafood import company, an upscale hotel, and a psychotherapy practice.

"You don't have to raise the baby with Ian. I'll help you. The million dollars is just a bonus." He leaned back, his gold-and-emerald cufflinks clinking, like a reminder of his wealth, on the chair's arms.

I shook my head. "I'm 44 years old! I have a teenage son. I'm a single mom. I live in San Francisco and you live in San Diego. And you are almost an octogenarian."

"Think about it," is all he said as he headed off to the bar for another Laphroaig Scotch whisky.

I stared after him.

Once again, the deejay played "Aïcha," my favorite song by Algerian raï artist Khaled. The enticing music and captivating rhythm chased Stanley's ridiculous proposition out of my head. The parquet dance floor beckoned. The disco ball spun out sparks of mosaic candy-colored lights.

As the night wore on, everyone in our party had retired except me and the deejay. He kept playing "Aïcha" as he watched me and smoked a cigarette. I had the entire dance floor to myself. On one of my twirls and swoops, I noticed another pair of feet. A lithe woman had appeared and was also swirling across the floor. She smiled at me. We immediately recognized each other as sisters united in ecstatic dance. A few Aïchas later, she took my hand and led me toward a table in the more secluded region of the club.

A man in a turban sat there studying us. He stood as we approached, put his hand on his heart, and said in a soft voice, "*As-salāmu alaykum*"—a greeting in Arabic that means "peace be upon you."

The woman introduced him. "This is my husband, Abdullah."

He was an elegant and gracious man. Tall, thin, chocolate-colored skin, gentle eyes. His turban was robin's-egg-blue and his djellaba or caftan, pearl-white.

"My name is Josee. I'm from Holland and Abdullah is Nubian. He only speaks Arabic. Please join us." She had a funny singsong Dutch accent similar to Julia Child's—like marbles were rolling around the words as she spoke.

As Josee patted the seat beside her, she asked, "Would you like some mint tea or a glass of wine?"

The disco ball scattered jewel-colored lights across Abdullah's turban and djellaba, giving him the appearance of a Gustav Klimt painting. I was surprised Abdullah didn't disapprove of his wife and me freeform dancing together. He appeared to be a devout Muslim, peppering his comments with *In shāa llāh* (god willing) and *Al-amdu lillāh* (praise be to god). In fact, that was the total of his conversation with me.

Josee wore a long, flowing, sleeveless dress like I did. She had cropped dishwater-blonde hair, no makeup, and did not wear a headscarf. "You two could be sisters." Abdullah smiled approvingly and nodded as Josee translated what he had just said. He seemed pleased with our budding friendship and mutual love of dance.

"Where do you live?" I asked.

"On Sahil Island in the Nile near Aswan. Abdullah is the village chieftain. We mostly live outdoors on a cliff overlooking the Nile, though I do have a small kitchen carved into the hillside and a tiny bedroom. But we usually sleep outside. We have no electricity so the stars are my ceiling. Across the water to the west is the Sahara. It stretches 3,600 kilometers, all the way to the Atlantic shores of Morocco. Sand and stars and turbulent waters inhabited by crocodiles surround us."

Living with crocodiles in the front yard got my attention. "Do you swim with them? I only have deer and squirrels on my property."

She chuckled. "Yes, we swim in the Nile on hot days but we keep an eye out for them."

After Josee translated my question about the crocodiles to Abdullah, who also found it amusing, she said, "Abdullah wants to know where you are from."

"I'm a fourth-generation San Franciscan and I'm traveling with my mother and five gay men. I've nicknamed our group the Queens of the Nile."

Josee laughed and didn't seem shocked, though I noticed she did not translate this for Abdullah.

"How come you are traveling with such an odd group?" she asked.

"Stanley organized this tour and invited my mom—she has a huge crush on him even though he's gay and she's married to my dad. She and Stanley are platonic best friends who often go on cruises together. Mom invited me to come to Egypt, so here we are—a weird dancing and prancing family."

"How long have you been married?" I asked, intrigued by this exotic duo.

Her eyes twinkled as she recounted their romance. "Abdullah and I met in Cairo. I was working as the communications director at the Groninger Museum in the Netherlands and visited Egypt on holidays. We married three years ago. Our wedding was on national TV because of our unusual story."

As the deejay dimmed the disco ball and packed up his music, I was about to bid my adieu when Abdullah motioned to Josee. She turned back to me and put her warm hand on my arm.

"Abdullah has invited you to join us in the captain's quarters. He and his crew will play music. Abdullah might sing. You should come. Nubians are renowned musicians."

I followed my new friends down a dark corridor to a private clubroom in the rear of the ship. As we entered, five men in gold-braided uniforms rose from their seats and bowed toward Abdullah. They seemed in awe of him and would not sit down until we were settled on the cream-colored couches. Abdullah was such a humble, soft-spoken man. I was curious as to why they treated him so reverently.

Everyone was silent. The captain raised an eyebrow toward the two officers holding doumbeks between their knees, and a soft finger tap on the rim of the taut hide of the ceramic drum led into a beat. The man next to them tuned his lute-shaped oud and began to strum, weaving his melody into their drumbeat. A faint, soulful wail came from another man who lifted a flute to his lips. The music rose like a cobra swaying upward from a coiled basket, twining with the other notes in a crescendo of Middle Eastern mystery.

Josee looked at me and asked quietly, "Do you like the music?"

Before I could answer, a haunting voice joined in, sailing over the instruments. It was Abdullah. I closed my eyes. The sound was beyond human.

A hush fell upon us and we leaned toward him, our faces turned upward. The officers silenced their instruments and Abdullah's song filled the void. He took us on a journey to a divine place where there are no boundaries.

Josee's soft whisper brought me back. "He only sings when inspired."

"Inspired by what?" I asked.

"God, Allah's presence."

"Tell me more, Josee."

She nestled back on the sofa and took a deep breath. "We were just in Holland visiting my parents. In a supermarket Abdullah spontaneously began to hum, which broke into a chant, which turned into a song. Everyone shopping came to the aisle where we were standing beside the coffee and pasta, and listened, hypnotized. When Abdullah feels the presence of God he gives it a voice, not caring where he is. It is bewitching."

I glanced at Abdullah, envisioning the scene, not doubting that I would have responded exactly the same way as the others had in that supermarket.

"We were invited on this inaugural voyage because the captain hopes he will sing, which will be a great blessing for this new vessel. Abdullah is viewed as a holy man."

With his eyes closed, Abdullah continued to croon. The only percussion accompanying him was the haunting noises of the ship creaking on the rocking waters of the trapped Nile. An undertone soon caught my ear—faint clicking sounds of leather heels. It was very late for someone to be wandering around outside. Then I saw the outline of a turbaned man with a rifle slinking past the window, silhouetted by the moon.

Noticing my concern, the captain leaned forward and whispered in my ear, "He is one of our watchmen who guard the boat at night from intruders."

This only enhanced my temporary sense of fear. Just two weeks before Mom, the Queens, and I departed for Egypt, 58 foreign tourists had been killed by Islamic militants inside Hatshepsut's Temple near Luxor. My dad and many of our friends counseled us to cancel the trip, but we followed my son's advice. "Don't let fear change your course." Even at the tender age of 16, he was so Obi-Wan Kenobi and an intrepid traveler himself. "Besides, tourism will be nil so you will have the sites all to yourselves."

Abdullah's voice brought me back to this room where we were safe, serenaded by sacred music. Just when the platinum face of the full moon dipped below the lake's edge, we said goodnight.

The next morning at the coffee bar, still mesmerized by the music from last night and captivated by the vision of Abu Simbel out the window with the sun rising behind it illuminating its grandeur, I eagerly sipped my latte. Just as the caffeine kicked in and I was plotting my day's exploration of this extraordinary antiquity, I heard Stanley greet my mother—excitedly telling her about his proposal to create an heir for his empire.

*Uh oh*, I thought. *This isn't going to go over well…*

With trepidation, I turned around and saw Mom's face blanch.

"You aren't going to do this, are you?" Her voice trembled as she looked at me in horror.

I patted her shoulder reassuringly. "Mom, Stanley is a mad scientist who just wants to create his ideal human." Of course, it was a bit different than most megalomaniacs' version as Ian was a kid and black and gay and I was past baby stage. I raised my eyebrows in warning at Stanley. "I don't think I can even have a baby now and I don't want one."

Mom's lips tightened into a thin line. My sweet, compliant mother turned on her beloved Stanley like a tiger. "What are you thinking?" she hissed.

Stanley was miffed, as he usually gets his way. He shrank back as if she might strike, and his demitasse cup rattled in its saucer as he put it down.

"Okay, okay. It was just an idea. A good idea…"

Smoke poured out of Mom's ears. I chuckled as Stanley slunk toward the breakfast buffet.

To distract my old-fashioned mom from her worries that she might have a grandchild fathered by a very black, flamingly gay man, I said, "I met the most lovely couple after you went to bed. He chanted in Arabic. It was divine. I hope you stay up tonight if he sings again—they would like to meet you."

Her eyes lit up. "What a dream! We must bring them a gift. Perhaps a bottle of rosé from Meknes, though I'm not sure if Muslims drink alcohol," she pondered, completely forgetting how angry she had been just a moment ago.

After breakfast we were allowed to wander through the temple on our own, unencumbered by guides or a schedule. Usually these UNESCO sites are inundated with tourists and the tour times are highly regulated, but since we were the only visitors, we had free rein to enter whenever we pleased. While all the other passengers were getting ready, I scurried the short distance across the hot sand so I could beat the herd.

It was dark and quiet inside. Giant bas-reliefs of Egyptian gods peered down as I wandered through the hall and toward the vestibule in the inner chamber. Not even a buzzing fly broke the silence. As I entered the vault, I felt an odd sensation at the back of my head, as though I was a kitten being carried by the scruff of my neck. A spiraling wave filled my body and I began to sway in a circle without losing my balance. What the heck? I could barely keep my eyes open; I felt drugged yet filled with pulsing energy. My arms rose of their own volition and I began to whirl in place. I was dancing internally and feeling as though I was being pulled upward, yet my feet were planted firmly on the ground.

Since no one else was there, and it seemed strange but not scary, I closed my eyes. It was as if information or knowledge was pouring into the crown of my head as I spiraled in a helical curve. It felt like a giant download of ancient wisdom or higher mathematical formulas or quantum physics.

Something beyond my understanding. Whatever—I was possessed by the geomancy of this place. Was I standing in a particular zone of syncretic ley lines or an energy highway? It didn't matter. I wasn't resisting the experience, as freaky as it was.

Suddenly, I was released back to my regular old self—standing in a windowless room carved into a sandstone mountain.

At lunch, served al fresco on the ship's deck, I didn't tell anyone about the experience. After we had finished our baklava and Arabic coffee infused with cardamom, I asked Mom to come back into the temple with me. She was psychic and I was curious if she, too, would be possessed by the energies emanating from the inner sanctum.

"Why do we have to go back now? I'm hot. I want to take a nap so I don't miss the music tonight."

"Come on, Mom, we won't ever be here again."

After a harrumph, she reluctantly followed me across the sand to the narrow doorway of the temple. The portal didn't even come to the knees of the colossal statues flanking it—four identical figures of Pharaoh Ramesses II sitting on his throne.

As the light faded and the air turned still and cool, we entered the second pillared hall, greeted by statues of guess who—Ramesses—and Nefertari, his wife, depicted as a third of his height. Every other deity or royal figure in the temple was much smaller in proportion to the pharaoh.

We passed through the vestibule and entered the sanctuary. I stood waiting in the same spot I had been in this morning, toward the back wall.

Waiting. Waiting.

I couldn't shake my expectation that something special would happen—that the magic of the place would reveal itself again.

Waiting. Waiting.

Nothing. Just Mom's restless scuffling as she paced back and forth, annoyed that I'd dragged her away from a nap. Abruptly, the supernatural vibes returned. This time I felt like a chess piece being moved across the board by giant fingers on my skull.

It directed me to the wall again where the statue of Ptah, a god connected with the underworld, awaited. It was in the darkness of this furthest recess that the energies were the strongest.

"Mom, come stand next to me," I whispered into the echoing shadows.

"Why? What's in that corner?" She walked over anyway.

"Close your eyes. Let's meditate together." Mom could relate to this because she had taught meditation in California.

As I felt the corkscrewing tornado-like sensation growing in the center of my head, I kept my attention on Mom. A smile alighted on her face. Her eyes were closed, and she was rocking back and forth. Her arms began to lift as she shifted side-to-side and I was worried she might tip over, but she didn't lose her balance. She looked like a prop plane trying to lift off on a windy day. The two of us were captivated by this vortex. I moved in a spiral and Mom kept her arms outstretched as she continued to sway.

I thought we had the place to ourselves until a voice broke our trance. "Phyllis, put your arms down. You look ridiculous. What are you two doing?"

It was Stanley, very annoyed to find us engaged in New Age woo-woo activities in the sanctuary. The psychiatrist in him had zero tolerance for occult phenomenon.

Mom was unruffled by his peevishness. "Stanley, come over here and close your eyes. You won't believe how powerful this place is."

"For god's sake, Phyllis. I don't feel a thing except chilly." It seemed like the energies that called to us were selective. No grumpy old gay men for their download! His tone made me think that maybe he was still stung by Mom's utter rejection of his million-dollar-baby idea. "This is embarrassing. I'm going back to the boat for tea. If you two don't show up by dinnertime I will know Scotty beamed you up." The shuffling of his Italian loafers receded as he walked away.

Mom grinned at me, her nap long-forgotten. She was hooked. It was like psychedelics without the consequences. I had no idea what was going on in this place, but it was real and site-specific and we both felt it. We hung out in the inner sanctum for hours, each in our own un-medicated orbit. Occasionally another member of our cruise would enter the chamber, but they all hightailed it out of there as quick as bunnies being chased by a coyote when they witnessed our peculiar behavior.

Much to Stanley's secret relief, we did show up for dinner. I think he was tired of wondering what we were up to and dreaded having to search us out again in some musty recess.

To my delight, Abdullah and Josee joined us at our table. A glass of rosé loosened my tongue and I shared in whispers with Josee our inexplicably mystic experience inside Abu Simbel. I didn't want any others from our entourage to hear, horning in and pooh-poohing the inexplicability of it. Josee's eyes lit up and she said, "I want to go with you tonight." She explained to Abdullah in Arabic about our secret evening journey into the temple, and he nodded his head, giving us a wink.

Josee turned to me. "Abdullah thinks this is a grand adventure but he will not join us. The music last night tired him out. Sometimes the singing depletes his energy."

First we had to sit through the tour's sound and light show. With our posse and a dozen other guests Mom, Josee, and I perched on benches, staring straight up at the temple's four enormous Ramesses statues fifty feet in front of us, lit in florid rainbow-colored lights. The overly dramatic Star-Wars-esque soundtrack boomed across the desert sands and rippled over the stillness of Lake Nasser. We waited patiently, sipping apéritifs, but when the last spotlight clicked off the three of us snuck back into the temple to our "launch pad," as Mom now affectionately referred to the power spot.

Josee was also sensitive to the spell the site had cast on Mom and me. With eyes closed, we all took flight and tripped the light fantastic. Stanley had gone to bed after the show, so there was no danger of him following and chiding us for our kooky trance dance.

Mom, Josee, and I had several more transcendent download dance experiences in various ancient temples. The grand finale was at the Temple of Isis at Philae, where we waited for our group and the other tourists to depart back to the boat before we danced and prayed and lost ourselves to the potency of the sanctuary where an image of Isis rested on a pedestal.

On the way out of the temple, I lingered behind Mom and Josee, not quite ready to leave the energy yet. Walking back out into the bright sun streaming through the colonnades, I spotted a red rose lying on the stones at the entrance. Its crimson petals, open and dewy-fresh, had not been wilted by the scalding sun. This flower hadn't been there when I'd entered. Scanning the landscape from the platform, I could see there were no rose bushes nearby and no one else was in the compound. Perhaps this beautiful blossom was a gift from the goddess Isis—maybe she appreciated my dance!

Stanley gave up trying to get us to act "normal and civilized." He even started to encourage our searches for those special magnetic places. Other people on the cruise were intrigued by our peculiar priestess-like behavior and, being a theatrical type and amateur actor, Stanley felt left out of being the star of the show. He didn't exhibit any ability to connect with the spirits so instead, he began to strut around, bragging about our magical talents, especially when I showed up at lunch with the rose and the tale of how it had appeared out of nowhere.

"Very abracadabra!" he commented, waving his napkin like the Queen's hankie. He immediately had the waiter bring a vase and placed my perfect rose in the center of our table for all to see. Later, Stanley pulled me aside and asked in an uncharacteristically shy tone, "Can I press it and keep it as a memento?"

On our return to California, Stanley bought the perfect trophy to capture the epic wonders of our trip to Egypt: a life-size replica of King Tut's throne. It was meant to be in the "Tutankhamun and the Golden Age of the Pharaohs" exhibit at the Los Angeles County Museum of Art, but it had a flaw so the museum auctioned it off to the highest bidder—Stanley.

The last time I saw Stanley was on his 80th birthday, shortly before he passed away. He threw a monumental party for himself. One hundred gay men and I sat in the banquet hall of his hotel in San Diego. Stanley sat on a stage in a caftan, regally perched on his throne with my elegant, silver-haired mother, wearing a silk suit and nervously clutching her handbag, seated on one side of him. Ian sat straight-backed in an embroidered opera cape on the other side, holding a staff.

My thoughts wandered back to our travels to Egypt together. What if I had taken Stanley up on his offer on that profoundly mystical night in a faraway land? I could have been Nefertiti sitting next to Godfather Stanley on that gilt and bejeweled throne, holding the million-dollar-miracle baby on my lap—a child who loves to dance and can sense the timeless energies that emanate from sacred places.

# THE CHILEAN CLIFF CARVER

Ibiza, Spain 1993

We met in a bullring under the velvet cloak of night. An evening lit by a pale pearl, bruised full moon. This was where I first encountered the pitch-black-haired Chilean who sported a smirk on his perfectly chiseled face. He stared at me while I was lifted to the heavens yet again. Not a human sacrifice but a contact dance performance I was hired to do at a private party on the island of Ibiza in Spain.

The Chilean and I skirted each other on the dance floor. Like matador and bull. I find attractive men dangerous and try to avoid eye contact with them. They terrify me.

Just as I did allow myself to look into his relentlessly piercing eyes, he swiveled and turned his attentions onto another woman. A real beauty. Slowly, they danced close together. Barely perceptible tendrils of steam were rising from their entwined bodies. He then danced with a man. He danced with the woman again. He danced again with the man. Then he danced with both of them at once. They were svelte and sensual, and wielded sly, flirty smiles. In my direction! Provocative. Especially in the flickering torchlight.

He came close again and grazed my bare arm. Red alerts were going off in my left brain. He looked like a heart landmine. Step toward him and my heart would surely be torn to bits.

This inner torment spiced up my dance routine with Oscar, my California dance partner, who seemed to be getting a little jealous that the Chilean was moving into his territory. Party guests were now standing in a circle around him and me, hemming us in as we increased the acrobatic lifts and spins. This hyper performance, fueled by alpha male competition and magnetic physical attraction, went on until the moon, exhausted, fell into the sea that caressed this limestone island in the Mediterranean. Wiping away the fine grit from the bullring that powdered my arms and face, I did not see the Chilean depart. He had vanished on the arm of another woman. Perhaps another man, too. For the best—I was not there to have a fling. I was there to perform.

My dance troupe did do more than dance on Ibiza. Several days after my encounter with the Chilean, in glaring sunlight, we went in search of the sunken civilization of Atlantis. Local lore had it located off the tip of Es Vedra, an island floating offshore Cala d'Hort's bay.

The scorching heat of the sun beating on the steep trail that led down to the bay released intoxicating herbaceous oils of wild rosemary, lavender and thyme that clung to the cliff side. When we reached the sea's edge, salt bream filled our nostrils. It was enlivening to be awake and outside during the daylight after so many all-night dance extravaganzas in Ibiza's uber-clubs and mega mansions.

As we leaned against the smooth, sun-bleached limestone boulders in this quarry on the sea's lapping edge, Sana handed each of us a ritualistic tab of ecstasy. Sana was our group leader and instigator of all things outrageous. As the zing zip of the drug effervesced in my bloodstream and my defenses dissolved, stifled emotions welled up. The secret burden of my life surfaced.

I had *so* wanted a little girl child. My son was adorable, but I wanted more kids. The abortion I'd had several years before due to my ex-husband's wishes was a sore, a gash still bleeding into my veins daily. As the heat emanating from the rocks penetrated my tense body, the iceberg-shard tips of that anguish melted and rivulets of sorrow slid down my cheeks pooling, in the hollow of my collarbone.

My maudlin grieving was interrupted by a shuffling sound. My teary eyes snapped open and there stood a young girl with long dark hair. Not a hallucination. Her jade green eyes stared directly into my sea blue eyes. By god, my wish was being granted. Who had waved the wand? Drugs are amazing. I'd always wanted another child, a girl to take to Paris. And here she was!

This little girl even spoke French. Her name was Marie-Claire. We bonded immediately. She grabbed my hand and pulled me up. She wasn't put off at all by the tears streaming down my face or my herky-jerky French. She wanted to play and to show me the crab.

Still holding hands, we walked past my bemused friends who could not figure out how I had suddenly conjured up a child, and waded into a tepid tide pool. She dove down, pale shiny child butt sticking up in the air. She popped up breathlessly and said I *must* do the same thing to see "him." Sure enough, once I did as she commanded, the crab was waggling his antennae eyes at me from under the rock through the murky water. Our upside down antics had stirred up the sand.

She then took me up a trail and around a ledge and we both peed on the dirt. Both of us were fascinated by the yellow streams gushing out from between our legs. Suddenly, hearty laughter startled us. On the boulders above us stood a man who was pointing and laughing. "Papa," she yelled, wagging her finger at him.

The Chilean! The dark handsome dancer from the bullring full-moon party.

For some reason, I wasn't self-conscious about having him see me peeing with his daughter, both of us totally naked. She explained to me that they had a camp beyond the rocks where he was standing.

Marie-Claire grabbed my hand again and ran down to the sea where the gurgling ocean waves sucked in and out over rocks covered in yellow-green algae. She beckoned me to sit on the green seaweed carpet and slide down into the water. A wave caught us and pushed us upward. We slid back and forth with the tide, laughing until tears ran down our sun burnt cheeks.

I'd completely forgotten my sorrows and desires. This happy child had invited me into her world, an enchanted playground of quirky sea creatures and hidden caves.

Then she slipped into the malachite green waters and disappeared. Her silhouette moved below the water's surface. She looked like a mermaid. Then, there was another larger shadow with her. I worried that it was a predator and dove in swimming to her depth. The shadow was her father. They didn't seem to need to come up for air. They showed me how to swim deep with the colder currents. These people were fantastical and mythical, dancing through their watery world like manatees or dolphins or selkies.

Marie-Claire was hungry after all her romping in the water and on land. We followed a narrow path that wound between the skyscraper-size Mesozoic boulders to where they were camping. He had created an other-worldly living space veiled in cream-colored canvas roofs, with thin slabs of pink slate as tabletops, white smoothed boulders for chairs, and Persian carpets that lay over the taupe sand.

The only way to get to their Bedouin-style encampment was by foot down the steep trail, or by Zodiac. As he prepared lunch, he told me he came here from Belgium every year and brought his boat and his daughter. They held court in this old-world quarry for the entire summer.

We grazed on large green olives, Manchego cheese, tomatoes, and fresh sardines. He had a soft yet radiant smile and told me his name was Patrice. He was from Dalcahue in Chiloé.

My mouth dropped open like an attic trapdoor. I was sitting in a dream setting of opaque rock and turquoise sea, without clothes, completely at home with a man who had terrified me several nights before. He was also blessed with a fairy princess daughter who was affectionate, intelligent and gifted.

Yet, this wasn't the reason my mouth was gaping open. It was because Patrice was from my favorite place in all of South America—perhaps the entire world. An island floating off the southern toe of Chile, only accessible by boat or seaplane, and only for six months a year when the savage winter storms subside. A place where the fishermen's wives knit bulky wool sweaters dyed in natural hues from the blood of walnut husks, moss, berries, seaweed, and mushrooms.

I knew Dalcahue well, as I went there many times in the 1970s to import those handspun sweaters. It took several days on planes, trains, ferries and small fishing boats to get there from Santiago, the capital of Chile. Nobody outside of Chiloé is from Chiloé.

His voice pulled me back to this island in the warmer climes of the Mediterranean. As he sliced ripe tomatoes on a stone slab, he shared that he was a ballet dancer and lived in a church in Brussels that he'd converted into an art and dance studio.

Damn!

Why couldn't he be pompous or stupid? Or from Milwaukee? This was all too delicious and tempting (and I'm not talking about the sardines!).

He flipped through a photo album and showed me pictures of his sculptural work. Full-size men and women engraved in the sand on the beaches of Normandy. Tides in the area shift, as described by Victor Hugo, "à la vitesse d'un cheval au gallop"—as swiftly as a galloping horse. The tide comes in at one meter per second. When the long tides were pulled in, Patrice filmed the encroaching foamy salt water eroding the Rodin-quality sculptures he had carved over many days. He chronicled the licking away at their curves, the dissolving of their shapes.

As he ran his fingers over the seashell-gray-toned photographs, describing the feel of the sand as he shaped these voluptuous bodies, his voice soft and faraway, I found him, his lifestyle, his family, all excruciatingly captivating.

## The Chilean Cliff Carver

A spell had been cast and I completely forgot about my friends back on the rocks.

In the late afternoon sun, after more explorations and a nap in their kasbah, Marie-Claire and I wound around the stones littering the hollow quarry pit they called home. There in the amber afternoon light, Patrice was squatting in front of a carving on the limestone face. It was a man and a woman embracing under water as they swam together. Botticelli delightful, da Vinci beautiful. Classic perfection.

As his golden arms and long-fingered hands chiseled these people into the rock, Patrice told me he was involved with the couple I saw him dancing with at the bullring. The sculpture depicted them. "It is complicated," he said. I don't know why he shared this with me but it made me feel very two-dimensional, simple, and boring. And American.

Suddenly, he looked at me mischievously out of the corner of his twinkling eyes and asked, "Would you like to spend the night? My daughter needs feminine company."

Maybe I wasn't so boring after all....

"What about my friends?" I asked in an embarrassing squeak. My vocal chords weren't cooperating. I was scared and looking for the exit. The intensity of the connection wiped me clean of sensibility and instead of feeling a resounding thunderclap *Yes!*, I practically tripped over him as I ran away. I didn't even say goodbye to Marie-Claire.

As I speed-walked past my astonished friends, who were halfway up the trail, one-way conversations bounced around inside my skull. *You would abandon your young son for a life with a bisexual, polyamorous man in cold, gray Belgium?* My mind spun out dramas as fast as it could to distract me from my attraction to this gorgeous man who had just invited me to spend the night with him. I mean, his daughter.

After I plowed over my friends to get in the car, they asked, "He invited you to spend the night? What are you doing here?"

I muttered something about them worrying about me if I didn't come back with them.

In unison, they all chanted, "Stupid! Isn't that what you wanted?"

On my last night in Ibiza, Sana choreographed yet another party. This one took place in an abandoned military fort. She turned each cold cement room into a vibrant temple celebrating various goddesses from Isis to Aphrodite.

Looking up from the flames licking the sky around the perennial bonfire ring, I saw his eyes across the fire's golden flicker. Panther eyes.

The Chilean and I skirted each other through the evening's mayhem of rituals and exhaustive dance-a-thons. I ended up collapsed in a sweaty pile next to him on one of Sana's makeshift temple floors. He draped a pashmina shawl over me as I pretended to sleep. No kisses. No hugs. No sex. No goodbye.

I arose at dawn and Oscar drove me to the airport for my long journey back to California.

I can still see the jaggy edge trim of his thick pitch-black hair framing his face. I can still feel the tidal pull of ultimate attraction. I'm still in love with that artist. Or at least the concept and packaging.

What if I had spent the night in that stone pink-tented wonderland he created? I muse about this every few years. What if I let the artist from my favorite remote island in the world woo me?

At first, I always repeat the same old litany, "No, no! I had to go home to work and take care of my son." But the blanket of reason that vigilantly guards the door to my heart falls off, and the truth speaks in a timid yet convincing voice, "I don't want to be swept away by the murderous riptides of love. No heart landmines for me (even if they are just in my imagination)..."

# DUSTING THE DANCE FLOOR

Ibiza, Spain 1993

"I can't go running off to Ibiza to dance!"

My proclamation comes out as a half-hearted whine. Sana has been dangling this invitation in front of me for weeks. She always rolls her eyes in disbelief at my very real and practical excuses for why I should stay home (work for example, family for example) instead of traipsing off to the dance film shoots, festivals, parties, and forays on dance expeditions she organizes. In her mind, ecstatic dance is the only reason to live and takes precedence over the more mundane details most people wrap their lives around.

Spontaneously dancing has been a condition I was born with. Dancing alone was okay; I'd gotten used to not noticing the critical gaze of the gawkers, most of whom wanted to be dancing too but just didn't realize it—yet. At least this is what I would think to shield myself from their mocking eyes.

In my mid-thirties, by some miracle, I found a tribe like me. People who knew that life *is* too short *not* to dance. Sana was the leader of this posse of colorfully dressed dancing dervishes who smiled as they swirled by in their own ecstatic movement exploration. Being surrounded by dancers who shimmied and hooted when the energy started to climb like a hawk on a thermal—that felt good. Synergetic. Supportive. Crazy good. It felt like I had come home.

Visions of dancers prancing through my head are burst by Sana's gravelly voice luring me to Ibiza to join the pack. She says, "I'll pay your way and all you have to do is dance every night in the clubs to stir up the floor."

The phone line is crackling with static. She must be in a phone booth on a street corner late at night in Barcelona or Havana or Amsterdam. Voices in a muffled foreign language punctuated by car honks, screechy wheels tractioning against cobblestones, all pepper the background noise.

"To do *what*?" I ask.

Sana's voice booms through the plastic receiver, "The German and British tourists don't dance. They just stand around like boring statues of Stalin and get drunk. Ugly drunk. The nightclubs in Ibiza are *over the top*. We are talking Olympic-size swimming pools in the middle of the dance floor and the *best* DJs in the world. The owners want floorshows and the DJs, brought in from all over Europe, want people to dance and express themselves, not be thugs and roily-eyed dopers. They will pay us to fly to the island and stir things up. Wear costumes, get wild, dance till dawn. What is there to say no to?"

She has a good point…

Ever since I've known Sana, she has led a nomadic life following the global party scene. She'd be brought in to create ambience at the big nightclubs in Cancun, Rio, New Orleans,

Berlin. She had a habit of linking in with places where dancing until dawn was a way of life. The woman was a migratory dance animal.

I met Sana Parker in Bolinas, a renegade whaling port on the northern California coast. She'd organized a summer solstice bonfire on the beach. Both of us naked, dancing with seaweed roped around our midriffs, seagull feathers woven in our wet hair, still damp from the dip into the freezing Pacific.

Her matted, calico-colored hair curled off her head like Medusa's snakes. Raggedy Anne aboriginal hair flying as she danced, water sprays arcing over the fire in slow motion droplets. She gyrated and swung her hair around like Rangda, the witch in a Balinese trance dance. Stars overhead, drumming, fire-lit shadows highlighting rounded breasts and drum-taut bellies, muscled men's broad ropey shoulders, fire opal hues glinting in the dancers' irises. It was extremely pagan. Sana's parties were legendary.

At first, she did not like me. I was too girly and the guys—she really liked the guys—were attracted to me, not her. She was almost like one of them, a female caveman type. Hairy armpits, loud voice, aggressive, opinionated, strong body odor, violent when she drank. No roses or prom corsages for that girl!

Sana and I were in an unconscious alpha female jostle that night in Bolinas, but we came to an understanding around the leaping and licking bonfire flames. We were both gypsy girls at heart.

The bond deepened and she camped out at my house in California every summer. She'd string a hammock under the fig tree and rarely come indoors. Unless she smelled coffee. She *loved* stimulants.

My ten-year-old son would call and tell me he was bringing friends home and request, "Could you tell Sana not to be outside naked when we get there?" She was naked a lot. Always doing some art project, naked. She painted our basketball court with psychedelic mandalas and dug a bonfire ring in the middle of it. She dove in the pool and then emerged, naked of course, shaking her mane out like a wolfhound. Entertaining for sure, but a tad embarrassing for a pre-adolescent boy to have to explain who the aboriginal person was with paint streaks all over her copper-toned body.

One time she asked a mutual friend and me, "What is your most sexy fantasy?" We responded with fairly normal scenarios. Her answer was a circle of men, laying on the ground, with her dancing in the center wet (and naked), flipping and slapping her tangled hair on their body. Tara and I looked at each other surreptitiously, *really*? No sex, no contact, except hair tips whipping nipples? No competition there! She could have that experience all to herself.

There is a reason she was paid to be the party maestro. She knew how to throw a party and proved it on her fortieth birthday, held at my house on a hot, cicada-throbbing August evening. One of the many spectacles that made it memorable was the large room she built outside on the front patio with two-by-fours and clear plastic sheeting. Fifty celebrants gathered around the structure. She was naked (surprise!) in the center with paint cans surrounding her. When the music started on cue, she lyrically swathed bold primary colors on the plastic walls with a house painter's brush and then danced against them, creating shapes and patterns with her face, fingers, breasts, and thighs.

This was followed by a tequila-fueled-bonfire-daredevil-wish-making ceremony on the basketball court that required all of us to take a swig, yell out our intention, and then do a running leap over the bonfire. Even my son. Move over, Tony Robbins!

There is a reason that even now, more than a decade later, when people are introduced to me, often their response is, "Wow! I went to a phenomenally wild party at your house." Wild was always the keyword surrounding Sana's behavior.

They then ask, "Do you remember me?"

I look at them, shaking my head, and apologetically respond, "Sorry! It was all a whirlwind blur of swirling bodies and sweat. And sometimes cops showing up to complain that people far across the valley could hear the drumming and hollering."

Sana's husky voice interrupts my reverie. The vision of Sana, glowing copper in a wave of movement, flickering around the many bonfires in our short but intense past, fades. She is impatiently awaiting my answer across an ocean of phone lines.

Getting far away from the man I am breaking up with, a possessive and jealous man, seems like a very good idea. Far, far away on an infamous island in the Mediterranean.

I relent, and my answer comes out as a big welcome exhale, *Yes! Buy me a ticket. I can leave immediately.*

We aren't the first wave of partygoers to find their way to Ibiza. In 654 BC, Phoenician settlers founded a port in the Balearic Islands 79 kilometers off the coast of the city of Valencia on the Iberian Peninsula in Spain. They named the harbor *Ibossim* (from the Phoenician *iboshim*, dedicated to the god of music and dance).

Since the arrival of the first muses, this island has been a destination for hipsters of legend from Joni Mitchell and Cat Stevens in the 1960s to Mick Jagger, Paris Hilton, and Seal nowadays. It has morphed into a hotbed for DJs who use the mega club scene in Ibiza as an outlet for presenting new songs within the house, trance and techno genres of electronic dance music. There also exists a genre of dance music named after Ibiza, dubbed Balearic Beat.

I don't know what to expect when I land on this mountainous island surrounded by a sapphire sea. But I pack my dance shoes.

Sana brings over six dancers from California to dance on the floors of Pacha, Amnesia, Es Paradis, Privilege, and Space.

The clubs don't really start cooking until one or two a.m., but the warm olive scented evenings seduce us into the streets of the old port of Ibiza Town, its ancient bone-white limestone buildings glowing in the moonlight.

During the day the town is deceivingly quiet. But at night the narrow streets are jammed with jetsetters and wannabes from all over Europe.

Sana has clutches of free club passes to handout on the streets. Of course, we don't just hand them out to the voraciously hungry club goers—we dance them out. In a giant rubber band. She came equipped with props! Hula hoops and gigantic gymnastic bands that could encompass a dozen maniac dancers. Sana is relentlessly unselfconscious and committed to our job of promoting the clubs that have paid our way to this pale alabaster island, epicenter of the global party scene. I have to work at it. The fun and endorphins always get me over the hump of *God, this must look ridiculous!* A bunch of adults in skimpy clothing, prancing through the streets in a giant rubber band expanding and contracting as we grab unsuspecting tourists, pulling them into the band with us like an out-of-control amoeba. At midnight, we dine on *mejillones al vapor* (steamed mussels in a pepper vinaigrette sauce) paella, and peasant bread dipped in garlicky aioli that we wash down with copious libations, including full-bodied Tempranillos and silky crisp Verdejos.

Then, as the moon glitters and winks at us across the harbor, we change into white-fringed dance costumes (more Sana props) and it is time to get to work. At Pacha, the über large bouncers (why do they all look like FBI agents?) lift the velvet rope, ushering us past the jostling throngs. We study the club layout and decide where the juice is needed. Stirred, not shaken is the idea, though shake we do. The DJs are really into the thump thump techno beat and it initially takes some creative internal convincing for me to feel that invasive, heart-stopping beat that overrides the normal body rhythm and increases the pulse. The club is the size of a sports arena and its sound system generates enough decibels that I'm sure the Moroccans are rockin' out across the water over in Tangier.

Our white costumes turn eerie blue under the pervasive black lights. We appear as floating sea anemones, transparent tentacles dancing Shiva-like through the awed crowds.

One night at Amnesia, Sana dives in the pool (naked) and swims back and forth with the beefy bouncers chasing her (they can't run very fast), yelling for her to put her bottoms on. Topless—okay. Bottomless—get arrested. Go figure.

People notice us in the clubs. Not just because of Sana's prowess as a swimmer, but because we are the only ones not standing around looking bored with a mega drink in our paw.

When our dance troupe isn't "dusting" the dance floor, as Sana likes to call it, we are invited to private parties at remote estates high up in the lonely hills on long windy gravel roads. Just as we start yawning and fidgeting in the cramped car, and wondering where the heck we are, lights suddenly appear and a home that has probably been featured in *Condé Nast Traveler* or *Architectural Digest* suddenly floats on a knoll in front of us. I can really relate to Cinderella arriving at the castle in a pumpkin, wearing ripped clothing.

Dancing always transports me to a magical place. The setting of this particular mansion in a park-like setting transforms me from a hard-working single mom, to a queen ready to alight from her dance throne.

A sweep of sparkling stars overhead lights our dance floor—an authentic bullring. Rich people need entertaining. Dancers, bullfighters, we're all the same.

This particular fairytale setting, with Moroccan Berber tents and Cleopatra divans set up around the dance ring, inspires Oscar, a member of our imported dance posse, and me to *really* dance. With passion and strength and vulnerability. No holds barred. The dozens of guests' handsome, chiseled faces highlighted by the torches are all turned toward us in stillness. Watching. Waiting. We blow them out of the water with our sinewy and sensuous acrobatic footwork and aerial dramas. Oscar lifts me and I slowly spin and flip over his back, my arms reaching aloft like raven wings, like Jesus on the cross, like peony petals lush in their exquisite flowering. The pantheon of stars inviting me to reach upward toward the *Little Prince* velvet night sky. Around my hips clings a crystal beaded silk scarf I bought from a belly dancer in Egypt. It refracts the starlight and tinkles softly as we dance up clouds of dust and dried blood. Our dirt dance floor *is* a real bullring. It has been for centuries.

We dance until the apricot sunrise laces through the dawning palette of a pastel sky. Oscar, Sana, Vision Dancer (yes, that is her real name), and I leave and go to a café. The thinly sliced *Jamón Serrano* (salty, dry ham) on chewy bread washed down with a café negro is divine after a night of continuous, sensuous, trance-like movement. The soft morning sun caresses our tired, upturned faces.

I don't see much of Ibiza during the day this trip. Except for the day Sana almost drowns. She pursues the crazy idea to swim three kilometers out to the legendary rock island of Es Vedra. By herself. There is a lot of mythology surrounding this rock in the sea. Some say it is the island of the sirens in the Homer epics or that it's the holy island of Tanit, a Phoenician goddess of fertility. UFOs are frequently reported landing here. Many claim it is the tip of sunken Atlantis.

Sana Parker did die a few years later when she was still in her forties. She was a pioneer of ecstatic dance, an enabler of free-form dancing. I can still feel her spirit dusting the dance floors at clubs and festivals around the globe. I'm pretty sure she is still not wearing any clothes.

# SPIRITUAL GRACE UNDER A BLUE BLACK SKY

Bali 1986

There is a dance tonight. There is one almost every night somewhere in Bali. I wrap a sarong around me, hold it up with a sash and wear a shirt that covers my arms. I do not want to offend the Balinese if the dance I'm going to attend should be held in a temple courtyard tonight.

I step out from my hut under a blue-black velvet sky set with sparkling diamond stars. The Balinese evening makes a sensuous tapestry. Incense, clove cigarettes and cooking spices mix with the heavy perfume of night-blooming flowers. The scents fill the still evening air and have an intoxicating effect on me.

Listening for a faint tinkling of music in the distance, I walk narrow dirt paths through the rice paddies. Deep-throated frogs keep time with my footsteps. Fireflies light my way.

The crash of cymbals becomes distinct, and the shadows of people appear, all wandering in the same direction. As I enter the village, kerosene lamps shine from doorways and catch the glimmer of gold threads woven into the sarongs worn on the lean, brown bodies of people moving toward the festivities.

We all head for the dance performance rumored to occur in this small village tonight, a night lit by a full blue moon. Its round face reflects in silver ripples on a multitude of flooded rice terraces, a moon that, as it rises, creates long black shadows along the path.

Among the surrounding villages, I've heard talk spreading about who would be performing at tonight's ceremonies. Will it be the humorous Topeng mask actor from Mas, the acclaimed dancer of the Kebyar from Peliatan, the particularly flirtatious and sinuous Oleg dancer from Ubud, or the young master of the Baris from the village where we are going tonight? Young and old come to see the classic dances they know by heart and have seen retold countless times in a hundred slightly different ways.

The *bale banjar* (community hall) is ablaze with kerosene lamps and alive with the hum and rustle of the village population milling about. We crowd onto hand-hewn wood benches to get a close-up look. I attract attention with my blond hair and blue eyes, especially from the children, who titter and flash me huge smiles. All of them have an appealing, mischievous twinkle in their eyes. Several matronly types approach and take the friendly liberty of retying my sarong properly. In their eyes I wrap it very awkwardly. Somehow, my big Western body doesn't look as graceful as theirs with this rainbow-hued cloth twisted around it. The fabric doesn't drape the same way on me as on their delicate frames. I am offered sweets and tea—no introductions, just village warmth. They are pleased a Westerner is interested in their village performance and has come showing respect by wearing traditional dress.

The gamelan orchestra warms up, and then, with a resounding crash, forty metal hammers hit the iron keys of the gamelan instruments in unison. This abrupt sound sends a jolt up my spine and seizes my attention. The trembling stage curtains part and out strides a Baris dancer in bejeweled attire, his feet stomping, eyes flashing and hands fluttering in rapid gestures. The movements of the Baris dance represent male strength, courage and resolve, the epitome of the warrior in the eyes of the Balinese.

Posturing brave stances with sweat gleaming on his brow, the young Baris dancer regally turns about and disappears. The music calms and softens; bells and the tinkle of the gamelan set the mood of the next dance. Fluttering fans appear from behind the curtains, followed by two charming butterfly-like creatures. The famous Legong dance has begun. The two tiny dancers sway and undulate, dip and turn, following the motion of their hand-held fans. These dazzling Legong dancers are the female counterpart of the Baris portrayal of the Balinese warrior spirit. They are like exquisite swaying flowers in full regalia of royal green and gold brocade. Crowns of frangipani blossoms frame their perfect features. Their delicate young bodies are bound tightly in swathes of rich silk.

These girls are chosen at five-to-seven-years-old for their attractive features and matching appearances. They are then trained in the manners of Legong. In the days of Balinese princely states, these girls were usually future wives of the rulers. The Legong dancers are viewed as the quintessence of femininity and grace in Balinese society.

The brilliance of the elaborate costumes, expressive masks and ornate headdresses combined with the well-trained, fluid movements of the dancers enrapture me. It is almost too much splendor for my eyes to behold, yet it is presented in such a simple setting.

This evening, like many other festival nights in Bali, features a potpourri of dances covering a wide range of styles, from comedy to masked tragedy to fiery, passionate depictions of love and war. The performers are as much actors as dancers, relying on eloquent facial expressions, often with very little movement of their bodies.

Dance is alive and flourishing in every corner of the island. There are more than fifty different dances and two hundred dance troupes. The villagers are proud of the arts, and this abundant creativity is shared with the community. The generosity of artistic spirit has inspired a fertile breeding ground for new versions of the dances as creative juices are plowed back into the soil of the community.

Most Balinese dances are created to appease and entertain the deities. The dramatic arts offer a means of cleansing the village by strengthening its resistance to harmful forces through offerings, prayers and acts of exorcism. Balinese dance strives to establish a middle ground—a harmony between two opposite poles. The moral message is clear to any Balinese child: good and evil are ever present; the fight for good requires the strength of a warrior and constant awareness of right actions, plus offerings to appease the deities on both sides of the fence.

Many dances include trance states. Trances are a common means for the Balinese to honor their gods by offering their bodies as vessels to the spirits and their messages. Probably the most spectacular of the trance dances is the Sanghyang Jaran.

For the Sanghyang, a large pile of coconut husks is lit in the center of the performing area. The burning mound of shells turns into a crackling fire emanating such intense heat that I break out into a sweat. When the embers are bright red, men spread the hot coals over the ground. The gamelan orchestra strikes a dynamic chord that makes me jump off my seat. The clash and clatter of sound announces the dramatic appearance of a barely-clad man on a wooden horse who gallops across the fiery carpet of glowing coals. We gasp again as he turns his stick steed about and charges once more into the heat. This time, he stops abruptly in the center, kicking burning embers in every direction. The dancer is overcome by his zealous trance state. He grins, then shouts and races this way and that, chasing evil demons that only he can see. His ecstatic fervor will go on until the priest recognizes that it is time to draw the man back to consciousness.

Another example of a dance performed tonight that invokes a devotional warrior state is the Kris (dagger) dance. Rangda, queen of the witches, is the most vicious and evil of the demon gods. Her straggly hair, pendulous breasts, and drooling mouth portray vileness. The she-witch enters the bodies of the Kris dancers, who represent the community. Under her destructive influence the men, in a trance, turn their own daggers against themselves. I find myself anxiously biting my nails as they dig the sword points into their bare chests. Again, the priest helps pull them back so that good may win. Then, the mighty Barong, protector of humanity and similar to a Chinese dragon in appearance, marches down the steps in the last scene to triumph over the nasty, horrifying Rangda and her foul cohorts.

The battle between light and dark is abated for the moment, and balance has been achieved between the opposing forces of good and evil. We exhale a collective sigh of relief. Children pile off the wooden benches, acting out some of the more gruesome scenes. We all gather around the food vendors waiting just beyond the halo of the kerosene lamps.

As I walk home late into the night, my hands flutter and arc casting dancing shadows on the ground, unconsciously imitating the graceful motions of those refined dancers.

# TWO-STEPPIN' AND PUSSY-POPPIN'

New Orleans 1977-1982

*Get up*
*Get up*
*Get up*
*Get on up*
*Stay on the scene*
*Get on up*
*Like a sex machine*

It was a rockin' night in the Big Easy. James Brown was belting out his classic funky song as sweat streamed down his animated face. His backup singers were howling, clapping, and shimmying. The horn section pointed to heaven, blowing and smoking as they fogged up the windows of the Delta Queen, a nineteenth-century paddlewheel steamboat. A tarnished copper moon cast rippling light across the water as we churned down the muddy Mississippi River. The frenzied crowd pressed right up to the stage like a rising tide.

And there I was, dancing and singing on top of the throbbing speakers on either side of the stage—best view in the house—making up my own lyrics because James was stuck on repeat. He must have chanted that same stanza a hundred times. Over and over.

*Get up*
*Get up*
*Get up*
*Get on up*
*Get up…*

This was punctuated with an occasional, "Like a sex machine!" or "Shake your money maker!"

Somewhere around the fiftieth repeat was when I started switching it up, singing with an unselfconscious *joie de vivre* that can only come from being well-lubricated on Tanqueray and tonic.

Until someone tugged on my ankle. Opening my eyes and coming out of my funky town trance, I looked down to see a black woman, who had hold of my leg and was shaking it to get my attention. "Shut up, honky!" she shouted, looking like she was going to bite. The sea of faces surrounding her also glared up at me. Was I being sacrilegious or off-key? I supposed either one was a possibility.

I knew I could shake my booty with the best of 'em, so that couldn't be why I'd stirred up a mob scene.

Must be my improvised lyrics:

"Get down."
"Don't get down!"
"Get funky, get real funky. "
"Oh heck, don't get funky."
"Get down."

"Get up."

"For god's sake, I said get down!"

Chirping like a canary, wailing like an opera singer. Keeping time with the man sporting the meringued pompadour—just whimsically altering the lyrics a tad.

Plus, I was busting a new move that a jiving group of twelve-year-old girls in cornrows taught me at the Jazz Fest. I asked them if this snake-like gyration had a name. It was a little disturbing to hear the young girls say, "Pussy Pop" without missing a beat. This sinuous dance step requires a very flexible spine and pelvis. Perfect for the King of Soul's anthem.

The sea of fans below me—all black except for me—did not seem to appreciate my vocal stylings or my *au courant* choreography. Fortunately, I was way off to the side of the stage and James hadn't noticed me...yet.

Okay, I was being passive-aggressive. James and I had a bit of history between us.

Now I felt a finger jabbing my other ankle not being prodded by an infuriated JB fan. I glanced down to see Lloyd Cottingim's bemused face trying to look annoyed with me, and failing miserably. Still, he scowled like an angry pirate and mouthed, "Get down!"

It was all Lloyd's fault that I was up here on these speakers, anyway. Well, not on the speakers. That had been my idea. My inner go-go girl was getting her mojo on. I'd just spent an eternity in the crowded, wire-laid backstage and was sick and tired of hearing the hot music licks without being able to dance.

The reason I was even backstage at all came back to meeting Lloyd, who convinced me to volunteer at the New

Orleans Jazz and Heritage Festival. I was charged with picking the performing artists up at the airport, taking them to their hotel, and then their gigs. The vehicle I was given to transport these mostly iconic performers was Lloyd's old but reliable red Chevy pickup truck. Not a limo. We were on a budget.

I had met Lloyd one night several years earlier in 1977, when I went out dancing by myself in San Francisco, where I lived. Clifton Chenier, a Creole French-speaking native of Opelousas, Louisiana, was playing at the Last Day Saloon on Clement Street.

I'd become infatuated with Zydeco music and Cajun dancing when a friend invited me to a black Baptist church. Not knowing what to expect, I walked into a whitewashed clapboard church packed with all ages and types of folks. On the stage was a projection screen, and we took a seat on the hard wooden pews in front of it. A man stood up and introduced himself. It was Les Blank, an ethnographic filmmaker from Berkeley. He was showing his documentary *Hot Peppers*, featuring a musical portrait of Zydeco king Clifton Chenier, and from the first scene I was hooked.

After the film, we pushed the benches away. Les and his friends ladled out red beans and rice in the back of the church while we danced to Clifton, who had driven out from the Big Easy for the occasion. I climbed feet-first onto the Zydeco bandwagon, dancing to Queen Ida, Buckwheat Zydeco, and Clifton whenever they came to the Bay Area and played at small venues like Ashkenaz in Berkeley, and at churches and community halls.

Now, at the Last Day Saloon, I stood in the dark and mostly empty club while Clifton wailed on his *frottoir*—a washboard made of corrugated metal and worn like a vest.

He furiously scratched the tin surface with spoons, cranking out Zydeco music. Tapping my foot for only so long, I got out on the dance floor solo. Several lively numbers later, I was joined by a short man with a devilish grin. He offered me his hand and away we went. He could Cajun two-step like a house on fire.

During the break, we propped our sweaty selves against the wooden bar and he treated me to my first Tanqueray and tonic. It was thirst quenching in a cold, limey, quinine kind of way.

In a thick Cajun accent reminiscent of warm maple syrup and butter pooling on slabs of cinnamon French toast, my dance partner introduced himself. "My name is Lloyd Cottingim. I'm from New Orleans. What brings you out to swing to Clifton by yourself?"

Taking a gulp of the tall, refreshing drink, I wiped the beads of sweat from my face and said, "This is dancing music and I'm a dancing fiend. Most of my West Coast friends don't groove to Zydeco."

Lloyd was a ship's engineer and had traveled to San Francisco from the Gulf via the Panama Canal. He told me he usually made it to San Francisco twice a year, and that he went to clubs, looking for live music, wherever he docked.

We danced till Clifton Chenier and his Red Hot Louisiana Band packed up their instruments and drove away in their beater van to the next gig destination. Standing on the sidewalk, still tapping our toes to a silent beat, Lloyd asked, "You want to eat ribs at the ocean? I have some leftovers in the car."

I wasn't attracted to Lloyd. He was troll-like with a scraggly beard, dressed in a faded plaid shirt, baggy jeans, and laced-up lumberjack boots. But I appreciated his Southern drawl, his gentlemanly ways, and his big heart. That night had shown me he was an outstanding dance partner with stamina to match mine. Plus, there was a mischievous spark in his eye, and he liked to have a good time. This turned out to be true for all the Cajuns I met, but he was my first so I didn't yet know how spunky and fun those swamp boys can be.

"Sure. I'm game—and hungry."

We hopped in his rental car and drove to Ocean Beach. Parked facing the crashing waves, we sucked on succulent, sticky ribs from Leon's Barbeque and listened to Keith Jarrett's jazz piano riffs on the tape deck.

By the time the sun rose, a pile of greasy napkins littered the back seat and we had embarked on a friendship that would last more than two decades. We shared a love of music, dancing, food, and conversation—and staying up till the wee dawn hours doing all of the above.

That same morning, over Dungeness crab benedicts and foamy lattés at Mama's in North Beach, Lloyd said, "You gotta come to Jazz Fest. I've worked for the Fest every year since it started in 1970. In fact, Clifton Chenier was part of our first lineup. So were Mahalia Jackson, Duke Ellington, and the Eureka Brass Band."

Lloyd looked at me expectantly, and I nonchalantly sipped my latté. I wasn't sold yet. He tried again, leaning in excitedly, as the café buzzed with early-morning diners.

"My job has gotten pretty hectic since the festival is growing exponentially each year. Three hundred and fifty folks attended the first one when it was held in Beauregard Square, and this year we expect over ninety thousand." He leaned back again, impressed by his own numbers. "It's gotten so big, it's now held at the Fair Grounds Race Course—a hundred-and-forty-five--acre site. Yeah, baby!"

"So what do you need me for?" I asked, a little suspiciously.

Lloyd folded his arms. "I could use an assistant. You can help chauffeur the performers around New Orleans and stay at my house. It's the end of April and goes for two weekends, but you should come for a month and I'll show you around Louisiana. It's like a foreign country."

I counted the weeks until April in my head—eight—secure in the knowledge that I could leave my retail stores in the trusted hands of my employees, and took a long, assessing look at Lloyd. Could I trust that he did not have an ulterior motive? I asked, "You serious? Even if it is platonic with no hope of me ending up in your bed?"

He chuckled and said, "No problem. I have lots of girlfriends. My bedroom skills make me popular with the ladies."

"Too much information," I said, rolling my eyes.

He added, a smile twitching at the corners of his mouth, "I'm fine with just being friends. You'll dig New Orleans and the Jazz Fest. It's Mecca for music hounds."

Lloyd would be true to his word and never tried to jump my bones. But I didn't know this about him yet. I just had to trust his generous and tempting offer. He'd already lured me with his fancy footwork and the late-night rib fest by the beach, and he knew my real weakness: dancing to live, soulful ethnic music until the early hours of the morning.

The next day I bought an airplane ticket.

Two months later, Lloyd picked me up at the New Orleans International Airport. He looked exactly the same as he did when I met him in San Francisco, except that he had traded in the long-sleeve plaid shirt for a wrinkly short-sleeve

Hawaiian number in a faded orange hibiscus flower print. He greeted me with a huge bear hug that lifted me off the ground, even though I was taller than him. His red truck idled at the curb.

First stop was Buster Holmes' restaurant in the French Quarter for red beans and rice with smoked sausage and turnip greens. Afterward we strolled down to Angelo Brocato's on Ursulines Street for cannolis and lemon ice. My initiation into all things New Orleans had begun. We then drove over to the Thirteenth Ward, where he had grown up near the Neville Brothers.

After pointing out the rickety double-shotgun-style house he was raised in and waving to a few old acquaintances hanging out on their front porches, sipping Barq's root beer from bottles, we cruised over to St. Charles Avenue.

"You don't mind if I do some work?" he said as we drove.

"Are we going to one of the ships you work on?"

Tossing the toothpick he had been cleaning his teeth with out the window, he said, "No. I'm also a city building inspector. I check out the historic houses that are getting a facelift and write up reports."

I was trying to figure out how he juggled so many diverse jobs at the same time when we pulled up to an ornate, tilted Queen Anne on the edge of the Garden District.

Lloyd got out and walked around to my side of the truck. The door was stuck shut, but it sprang open when he gave it a hard, noisy kick with the same lumberjack boot he was wearing when I met him on the dance floor in San Francisco. We sauntered up the crooked wooden steps and he knocked.

Heavy, shuffling footsteps and a high-pitched voice trilled, "Don't let the cat out!" The door creaked open. A statuesque, barefoot man in a black silk kimono embroidered with chrysanthemums greeted us, just as a fat tabby ran between his legs and escaped onto the street.

"Lloyd! My *favorite* city employee! Are you here to check my pipes?"

Lloyd blushed. "Armand, you are such a tease! Meet my California assistant. She flew all the way here from San Francisco to help me at the Fest. It's her first one."

Clapping his hand to his forehead, Armand said, "Oh my, a Fest virgin. Be prepared for one crazy time if Lloyd is in charge of your itinerary. You won't be a virgin for long!"

As Armand leaned forward to grasp my hand, his kimono fell open, revealing a hairy chest, six-pack abs, and a g-string.

"Where's my belt?" Armand fussed as he waved us inside. "Would you like chicory coffee with a dollop of Baileys Irish Cream, or gin martinis?"

Though it was early afternoon, the drawing room was dark with its heavy, red velvet curtains drawn and crystal chandeliers shedding dim light. Large gilt mirrors reflected our shadowy, distorted images. I felt small and ordinary compared to our host, who was still clucking and chuckling about me being a "virgin." Lloyd went to check the kitchen remodel and I sat across from Armand on a leopard-print divan. He had still not belted his robe shut as he poured martinis into three bathtub-size glasses.

We toasted to my first Fest and then Armand gushed, "Tell me all about Frisco! In the 1960s I performed there at Finocchio's on Broadway in a drag queen revue."

Two hours later, we stumbled outside into the stark sunlight. I squinted at Lloyd and asked, "Are all the homeowners of the houses you inspect such hospitable characters?"

As he giddily skipped down the steps a bit lopsided, he said, "I pass every building permit application. I know everybody in this town. How can I not help them out? I get a lot of perks, too. From coffee cake to cash; sex to music." He winked and nodded toward Armand's house. "Even martinis!"

We drove to several other houses in the Garden District and Lloyd explained their architectural styles and history. "This was the biggest Confederate city in the South. Barely a year after the Civil War started, New Orleans was captured without combat or bombardment. As a result, we have the largest collection of surviving Antebellum architecture."

These architectural grand dames kept company with enormous, ancient oak trees that spread protective, leafy arms over charmingly disheveled gardens hedged in rhododendrons, azaleas, and camellias. Dark-leafed magnolia trees in full bloom shed handkerchief-sized ivory petals on the emerald-green lawns. Lloyd pointed to a Victorian painted a lurid lavender and said, "This home was built in 1857 for a wealthy merchant, who shot and killed himself on the front porch after running into financial trouble." He pointed to a throng of people looking up at the house. "That group of tourists milling around on the sidewalk are on a 'haunted house' walking tour."

Just as we slowed to a stop in front of the Victorian, I heard the guide announce to his flock in a tremulous tone, "I have seen a misty form float across the front porch, so keep your eyes unfocused yet focused."

I laughed and said, "I'm surprised the tour is during the day."

We continued on to the funkier Marigny and Bywater neighborhoods on the other side of the French Quarter,

## Two-Steppin' and Pussy-Poppin'

stopping at hulky Greek Revivals and narrow shotgun shacks made from swamp cypress during the Civil War era that were on Lloyd's inspection list. Most of the owners or contractors weren't home, so he left chatty, hand-written notes on their door, each signed with his curlicue signature and a happy face. He certainly didn't act like any government official I'd ever met.

Getting back into the truck with a groan after his last stop, where they plied us with hot, sugary beignets, he said, "How about I take you to the Jazz Fest offices and introduce you to the staff? If we're lucky, Gus will be deep-frying his famously tasty turkeys."

Balancing out the martinis and beignets with substantial food sounded like a good idea. It was beginning to occur to me that I would have to throw my regular California diet of fresh, organic salads and whole grains to the wind while here in the Deep South.

The office at the fairgrounds was in chaos. The frantic staff was juggling all the last-minute logistics of running one of the most popular music festivals in the world, with bands flying in from as far away as Senegal, Belize, and Madagascar.

Lloyd pushed open the screen door and said to everybody in the makeshift trailer office, "Meet my volunteer assistant from San Francisco."

Quint Davis, the Fest producer, came over and I felt an immediate attraction. His sleeves were rolled up and he was talking on two phones at once and rolling his eyes, but managed to give me a warm smile. He handed the phones to a staffer and said, "Welcome to the hub of the bedlam! We're all meeting up at the Rock'n'Bowl later tonight. Why don't you join us so we can all get to know you a bit more?" I nodded, grinning. "Good!" he said. "Now, it's back to work."

My palms were sweaty from the encounter with Quint and the humidity. I turned away and followed Lloyd over to his desk. He picked up the roster of the musicians we'd be shuttling between the airport, their lodgings, and performance venues, and I looked over his shoulder and whistled. It was a veritable *Who's Who* in the music world: Dr. John, Duke Ellington, Youssou N'Dour, Branford Marsalis, Linda Ronstadt, Miles Davis, Aretha Franklin, Tito Puente, The Temptations, Ella Fitzgerald. "Who *isn't* on this list?" I said. Lloyd raised his eyebrows, his grin practically saying, "I told you so."

A tantalizing, meaty aroma emanated from the parking lot. Distracted, Lloyd handed me the clipboard and went outside where a hefty man wearing overalls, with a sweaty red face, auburn hair, sideburns, and a beard, was prodding a rotund turkey that bobbed in a boiling vat of fat with a long, metal fork. The fryer was a custom-made behemoth that looked like a locomotive belching savory-smelling smoke.

"Hey Lloyd, what's up?" the man said and slapped Lloyd hard on the back.

"Easy, Gus, I don't want to fall in the fryer." They both guffawed in that wheezy geezer-guy way, like what he said was the funniest thing they'd both ever heard. Lloyd nodded to the bird. "Got any turkey ready to eat for me and my friend?"

"Yeah, go on inside my trailer. There's a hot platter piled high. Help yourself. Cold Jax beer is in the fridge."

The trailer was dark. I tripped over two German Shepherds huddled together, gnawing on turkey legs. They gave a low growl, scurried under the dining table, and continued demolishing the bones with loud crunching sounds.

We crowded around the Formica table, careful to keep our feet away from the dogs, and dug in using paper towels for plates. Lloyd grabbed a drumstick and said, "I could devour an entire tom."

"So what's Quint's story?" I asked, trying to sound casual, while Lloyd inhaled his food.

After he swallowed, he cocked his head and raised an eyebrow. "Interested, eh? Don't get your hopes up; I think he's engaged to Linda Ronstadt."

I giggled nervously. "Oh, well. Don't think I'll win that contest."

After he had polished off the platter and two beers, he burped and I asked, "Why does Gus fry the turkey?"

Lloyd leaned back against the banquette and said, "He insists baked turkey is too dry and bland for Cajun tastes. Unlike roast turkey, a quickly cooked deep-fried turkey is rich in flavor, with a crispy, golden-brown skin and tender, juicy interior."

Mouth full of the delectable meat, I could only nod my head in agreement as Lloyd continued, "Gus McIlhenny's family has been making Tabasco Sauce since 1869. He lives on Avery Island and is heir to a huge fortune. But all Gus really wants to do is live in this trailer with his dogs and fry turkeys for his friends. He loves feeding people!"

Licking the salty and spicy grease off my fingers, I exclaimed with a satiated sigh, "That was the best turkey I've ever eaten. What's Gus's marinade?"

"Well, it's a secret. He won't share the recipe with anyone. Even for front-row Rolling Stones tickets…I tried. I suspect it includes a lot of his family's red-hot pepper sauce."

We threw our bones under the table to the voracious dogs and went outside to thank Gus, who was busy trussing another turkey for the fryer.

"See you at the Rock'n'Bowl," Lloyd yelled through the office screen door.

We headed back Uptown to take a nap before going out dancing, making one pit stop to nab a few slices of oozing pecan pie topped with whipped cream at the Camellia Grill, down the street from his house on Carrollton Avenue.

As we clumped up the rickety staircase to his front door, an elderly woman in a faded flower-print nightgown leaned out of a second-story window across the alley. An ashy cigarette dangled from the side of her mouth.

Lloyd waved. "How you doing today, Miss Ermaline?"

Bleary-eyed, she hacked and said, "Peachy, Lloyd. Thanks for askin'."

She stared at me, shaking her head. "Who's the new girlie you got there? And why is she following you around with a clipboard and a suitcase?"

"She's my assistant."

Ermaline humphed and said, "Right... and I'm your chauffeur." With a sly cackle, she added, "Got any pot?"

Once he reached the top of the steps, Lloyd rummaged around in his briefcase and yelled, "Catch." He tossed Ermaline a baggie, which she snapped out of the air like a gator swallowing a leaping frog.

"Thanks, Lloyd. You can deduct it from my next paycheck." She giggled girlishly, then disappeared inside and shut the window with a thud.

"Well, I won't be seeing that money any time soon," Lloyd grouched.

Why did I get the feeling this was another of Lloyd's "jobs"?

Ermaline wasn't the only one who loved her marijuana. After Lloyd got me set up in the guest bedroom, he went into the living room. He sat in his great-grandfather's rocking chair, placed an upside-down shoebox lid on his lap, and neatly rolled several thin joints, all the while rocking back and forth. The inch-deep grooves in the hardwood floor were evidence that this was where he had spent several decades rocking and rolling, smoking and reading. I discovered that Lloyd was a night owl and barely slept; hence he was one of the most well-read people I'd ever met. He was filled with facts and details on a myriad of topics—a human encyclopedia. It was one of the reasons he was such a good conversationalist.

That night, we sauntered down the street to the Rock'n'Bowl in the warm evening air faintly scented with river detritus and night-blooming jasmine. Even though I was tuckered out from our gallivanting around town and didn't really want to bump into the possibly engaged Quint, Lloyd insisted that I hear Professor Longhair—yet another New Orleans legend.

"How could a music club be in a bowling alley?" I asked. "Won't the crashing pins and bouncing bowling balls drown out the music?"

Lloyd shook his head and hooked his finger, motioning me to follow him inside the noisy club. Downstairs was well-lit, with several groups of people queuing around the lanes. Upstairs was dark. There was a stage and a dance floor with chrome tables scattered about.

It was around midnight, and an elderly man sat on a piano bench muttering to the audience. He wore sunglasses and was hunched over the upright piano. He began to play and the place lit up. This skinny old man with the gold-toothed smile rocked the house with his Mardi Gras second-linin' music—his fingers rolling, hopping, and pecking over the keys like jumping beans. We pushed the tables aside and cut loose. Along with Lloyd, there was a plethora of great dance partners who kept me two-stepping to every hot number.

Our dance-a-thon was interrupted when Professor Longhair suddenly stopped playing. We all turned around in mid-step and saw that a woman had gotten on stage. We heard her ask if she could sing with him, and he nodded and began tinkling the keys. The woman joined in. It was the unmistakable voice of Rickie Lee Jones.

None of the Jazz Fest staff ended up coming that night, but who needed them? Any thought of Quint Davis was danced out of my mind, accompanied by the sweet musical coupling of Longhair and Jones.

These impromptu jam sessions happened night after night at every club we went to. Lloyd was right: New Orleans was the mother lode for live music. Add to the mix all the stellar musicians performing at the Jazz Fest, who then spontaneously dropped into the clubs for a spot of improv, and it was pure overload.

My job started the day after my first experience at the Rock'n'Bowl with a run to the airport to pick up Flora Purim, the Brazilian jazz singer. I already had her solo album and was nervous to meet one of my main divas. She was unmistakable as she glided into the arrival lounge in a long, white cotton dress, her many bracelets jangling. I introduced myself and she sashayed after me toward the red truck. For once in its creaky, rusty existence, the door opened effortlessly. She lifted her flowing skirt and lithely hopped onto the bench seat. I was worried she might be put off by our outdated wheels but she rolled down the window, turned to me with a broad, sunlit smile and said, "I love Louisiana already!"

She chatted about her life on the drive into town, and white cranes flew over the truck when we drove along the Lake Pontchartrain Causeway. "Oh, such a good omen!" she exclaimed delightedly. The briny smell of shrimp and brackish water floated in through the open windows.

Her soft, lilting accent soothed my discomfort with being so close to one of my favorite singers. "Are you hungry?" I asked. Her performance wasn't until that night. She nodded.

We drove straight to Buster's, where Lloyd had introduced me to red beans and rice just the day before. It only cost a dollar a plate, but they were the tastiest beans in the South. Flora said, "This dish reminds me of *feijoada*—Brazilian bean stew." Sweat beaded on the icy beer bottles as we feasted and yakked about our travels.

Flora and I hit it off. I had hitchhiked through Brazil in the early 1970s and spent two weeks dancing in the streets of Salvador da Bahia during Carnival. We had a lot to talk about.

We drove to the hotel and later I picked Flora up and took her to her performance. She extended her trip three extra days and asked if I would show her around town. I told her we could discover New Orleans together with Lloyd's guidance. After nights of clubbing, during which Flora got on stage to warble with Irma Thomas; Dr. John; and Rockin' Dopsie, Jr. & The Zydeco Twisters, we'd eat greasy pre-dawn breakfasts at the Hummingbird Grill, a twenty-four-hour diner in Skid Row where sleepless heroin addicts sniffled over their coffee. I dropped Flora off at the airport and she invited me to her and her husband Airto Moreira's show in San Francisco a month later.

I was developing a reputation at the Fest office of being an exceptional shepherd to the musicians. Lloyd was very proud of his acolyte. After the festival ended, I flew back to California and my busy life, promising Lloyd I'd come back and work for him again. I kept that promise five years in a row.

On one of my annual visits, I got assigned to escort Cab Calloway around town. It was a big day for me. I'd watched him dance and sing on The Ed Sullivan Show in 1967, performing "Minnie the Moocher." Looking slick in a white tuxedo, he'd scat-sing while doing a gliding backstep—the precursor to Michael Jackson's "moonwalk."

He was shorter and greyer than I remembered when I met Cab at the airport, but still debonair decked out in his trademark tuxedo.

He didn't blink when I ushered him out to the red truck. He graciously opened my door, then went around to his side. Miraculously, the door cooperated without the usual persuasive kick. Cab lifted his tails and swept onto the seat.

As with Flora, I developed an immediate friendship with Cab. We'd sit in the cool, dark recesses of his hotel lounge, sipping cocktails, and he'd regale me with insider stories of the jazz world from the 1930s when he played in Duke Ellington's band and headlined at the Cotton Club—New York's premier jazz scene. As I nibbled on a syrupy maraschino cherry, Cab's seductive, smoky voice wove a cocoon around me, revealing another era of cigarette holders and furs, big bands and Bing Crosby. Then we'd go to the Maple Leaf and eat a dozen raw oysters at the bar for ten cents apiece while listening to Aaron Neville croon "Tell It Like It Is."

Before I drove him back to his hotel, we'd stroll under the moonlight, looking beyond the levee at the silvery fish-scale whitecaps flitting across the Mississippi. The river was six feet higher than the street, and the only thing between us and being under water was a packed-down pile of dirt. Cab and I would shake our heads and marvel at the feat of engineering keeping all that water at bay.

On my very last trip to the Jazz Fest in 1982, I found the atmosphere of New Orleans had changed.

That year Laura, Lloyd's new wife and the head of operations for the Jazz Fest, picked me up at the airport. Lloyd was busy chauffeuring Dizzy Gillespie around town.

I'd be staying at their new home in Algiers Point—a free ferry ride across the river from the French Quarter. Before I even settled myself in the front seat of the faithful ole red truck she said, "Promise me you will not walk by yourself everywhere at all hours like you usually do. This town has gotten really dangerous."

At a stoplight on Decatur Street, Laura reached into her purse and showed me her handgun.

I raised my eyebrows. "Since when did you start carrying a gun?"

"Since crack cocaine showed up on the street," she replied matter-of-factly.

Just then, a hulking man in a shiny tracksuit threw himself across the hood of the car. Gripping the wipers, he pressed his acne-scarred face against the windshield. Several teeth were missing. Wild-eyed he screamed, "Bitches!"

"See what I mean?" Laura said calmly as she tromped on the accelerator.

The crazed man bounced off the hood like a ping-pong ball and rolled back into the gutter.

Laura didn't break a sweat—or glance in the rearview mirror.

She said sternly, "You will not go out at night by yourself! Capiche?"

I did go out that night with Lloyd and Laura for a seasonal treat of soft-shell crab meuniére at Mandina's, and then on to Tipitina's to dance ourselves sweaty-silly to the drunk and opiate-laced powerhouse Etta James. Her bawdy lyrics made me blush.

The next morning, Lloyd shook me awake. He waved croissants and black coffee under my nose as I rose from the creaky couch. "Get up, lazy. James Brown is arriving at the airport in one hour and you're picking him up."

I got there just as the plane landed. I waited and waited. Everyone had debarked and departed. The only person left in the deserted lounge was a short, older woman wearing a maroon pantsuit with sturdy pumps and a handbag. Swiveling her head in all directions, she turned and made eye contact with me. She had a creased, mahogany face framed by a bouffant hairdo, and looked vaguely familiar.

Then it struck me. That was the same face on the cover of James Brown's *Sex Machine*. An album I played incessantly when I was a teenager in 1970.

It must be his mother or… "Mr. Brown?" I hesitantly queried as he turned again and stared at me in disbelief.

"Where's my driver?" he screeched without bothering to say hello or ask my name. He looked poised to hit me with his shiny patent leather handbag.

Trying to keep the welcoming smile from sliding off my face, I politely said, "Sorry, I didn't recognize you from the back, but I do work for Jazz Fest. I'll be taking you to the hotel."

This did not soften his dour expression. Taking a deep breath, I turned and walked outside to the curb. Though boiling mad, he followed me to the truck, and I opened the door with only one well-aimed kick.

He looked horrified and squawked, "You're just a girl! You can't be my driver, and this jalopy can't be my ride. Where's my limo?"

Somehow, I herded him into the truck. I tried to strike up a conversation but he didn't say another word on the drive into New Orleans, although he made a lot of huffy noises and kept patting his stiff hair back into place. The windows were wide open, as the air conditioning didn't work. With great relief, I dropped him off at his hotel.

Later, I heard from the Fest management and stage crews that he was indeed a demanding pain-in-the-ass. He also made a point of telling them he did not want to be chauffeured around by "that girl in the truck."

I didn't have the pleasure of encountering Mr. Brown again until my night dancing on those speakers, cruising down the moonlit Mississippi.

Temperamental pain-in-the-ass he might be, but I had to appreciate his showmanship and ability to work the crowd into a froth of moaning, gyrating, screaming, and Pussy Poppin'.

*Get on up*
*Get up*
*Shake your arm*

*Then use your form*
*Stay on the scene like a sex machine.*

As he *finally* ended the song and the sex machine ground to a halt, I sheepishly slid off the speakers and slunk backstage out of sight, Lloyd shaking his head after me. After all, that crowd was there to see the King of Soul, not the honky from California. He may have been a huffy, cantankerous grandma with me, but for them, he was the original sex machine.

# THE SAN FRANCISCO DANCE LADY

San Francisco 1974

I thought the crunchy, nibbling noises were rats between the floorboards.

Then, in the silence of night, I heard my roommate Renée retch. I descended the loft ladder to check. Hunched over the toilet as small as a pale rabbit, Renée vomited—her thin rib cage heaving like an overworked accordion. I slipped my hands under her armpits, lifted her away from the porcelain rim, scooped her up, and carried her to the futon in our living room dance studio. Renée weighed nothing; she was bulimic. I did not know about eating disorders.

Crumpled on the kitchen floor was a family-size box of Rice Krispies. Empty. Renée was the rat, living on desiccated breakfast cereal. In the shadowed light drifting in from the streetlamp in the dark of night it occurred to me that in the entire week I'd been living there, I'd never seen her eat during the day. The refrigerator was empty. The cupboards were bare. Now I understood why—she only ate Rice Krispies.

Chinese takeout was my sustenance. We lived in the heart of San Francisco's Chinatown on Clay Street. I dined on glistening tea-smoked duck, emerald-green steamed broccoli, succulent shrimp balls wrapped in rice noodles, cashew chicken in gravy with fresh peas, carrots, and crisp water chestnuts. An affordable feast surrounded our neighborhood. Heaven for a voraciously hungry 21-year-old on a scant budget. Shopping in Chinatown was a zoology lesson—I'd avert my eyes at the tubs of live turtles and frogs trying to escape their inevitable end in the soup pot. Writhing eels occasionally flipped their slimy, speckled bodies out of the barrel and slithered between shoppers' legs, heading toward the tourists waiting for the cable car. The out-of-towners squawked and scattered like alarmed seagulls.

Late at night, walking through the empty streets of Chinatown after dancing in clubs, Renée showed me how to steal cabbage from the overflowing produce trucks parked along Stockton Street. The football-shaped cabbages were easier to tug out from between the wooden slats than the broccoli—and we'd only take one. Just one. I ate the frilly yellow-green leaves raw.

Living in this Asian warren—where we were the only resident Caucasians—cost literally nothing. Rent was free due to an unusual agreement Renée had with the eccentric landlord. I was scraping together funds for a two-year journey to South America, and needed to save every penny from my job at Warner Electra Atlantic.

Dancing didn't pay. Well, sometimes it did. Renée would regularly get peculiar performance contracts and included me in the deal. One Saturday afternoon, I hopped into her borrowed clunker. She wouldn't tell me where we were going.

We drove across the Bay Bridge and exited at the Alameda tunnel.

"What? Where is this job?" I asked, beginning to wonder about her latest escapade. Usually we got gigs dancing at wild parties for coked-up rock stars in swanky Marin County homes.

Renée ignored my question and said, "We each get $50 to dance for an hour." That quelled my concern. It would cover a third of my airfare to South America.

Did you know that men still yell, "Take it off!" in strip clubs? But this wasn't a strip club—it was the Alameda naval base officers club, where I assumed men had manners. The manager said he hired us specifically because we didn't dance naked. "The last gals got fired because they couldn't keep their clothes on. No matter what these guys offer you, *do not strip!*"

I wasn't planning to but the men at the bar, all in officer uniforms, were disappointed as I dipped and spun to the 45s on the jukebox. They started hooting and waving dollar bills like testosterone-fueled baboons, thumping their fists on the bar and commanding, "Take it off!" I couldn't wait to get out of there.

"What a bunch of pigs!" I told Renée an hour later, after we collected our payment and scurried back out into the dim, fog-lit afternoon.

Dancing did meet our basic monetary needs, but not doing so for a bunch of goons. Renée had a patron who kept a fatherly eye on her: Tony Serra—a civil rights lawyer for Black Panther leader Huey Newton. A highly controversial figure, he didn't pay taxes, had spent time in jail, and only represented rebels, pro bono. They even made a movie about him—*True Believer*, starring James Wood.

Tony not only paid our rent, he occasionally took me out to dinner. Renée never joined us due to her late-night cereal binges. He inducted me into the exotic world of sushi and wasabi, where he practically snorted the fiery green horseradish along with other drugs of the white powder variety—right at the sushi bar. Both substances made his eyebrows wiggle like hairy caterpillars, his eyeballs cross, and a zany grin spread across his gypsy mug. *This guy really is a rebel with a cause…albeit missing some teeth,* I thought as I watched him process the green stuff. Then I tried the wasabi and *whoa*! My eyes watered, my nostrils burned. My brain was on fire.

"This is food—not gun powder?" I asked Tony.

Instead of an answer, he handed me a rolled-up dollar bill and pointed to the inch-long line of cocaine he'd chopped on the counter. I declined. I was still a naive drug virgin and that powered Japanese condiment was mind-blowing enough.

Once or twice a week, Tony brought his entourage over to our studio—probably famous people I would have recognized if I'd been paying attention. The men sat on cushions spread out around a low coffee table, smoking hookah pipes, and drinking tea while they discussed politics. I'd hear snippets: "Russell Little, Hells Angels, Bill Graham, SDS, blah blah blah." It meant nothing to me. I was a globetrotter—not an activist.

In between heated discussions, they'd watch us frolic across the wood floor. Tony had endowed us with a record player and vinyl collection. We were not expected to get sexy or be alluring—just do an etheric dance to hippie tunes: "Nights in White Satin" by the Moody Blues, "Dancing in the Moonlight" by Van Morrison, "White Rabbit" by Jefferson Starship, "Fly Like an Eagle" by Steve Miller Band. Our audience smiled and nodded approval; not a lecherous grin in the group. It was all very innocent. Except for the bong, I guess...

As they puffed, Renée and I channeled Isadora Duncan. Renée was a contortionist, so her moves included yogic backbends. While I fluttered about tamely in my diaphanous nymph outfit, flitting a silk scarf in arcs over my head, she'd bend backward in a horizontal position from the waist up, still dancing and moving gracefully, seemingly defying the laws of gravity. It was a hypnotic, almost otherworldly thing to witness.

Sometimes, I'd stop and stare in awe at her latest improbable maneuver. There was no sense of competition as we both knew scarf-waving was my specialty. I could barely bend forward to touch my toes, but we shared a sincere love of dance. With our long blonde hair, we looked like sisters, except I was six inches taller and twenty-five pounds heavier than the waif that was Renée. She was a sprite; I was a filly.

I first encountered Renée at the record company where I worked—Warner Electra Atlantic in the Cannery.

It was lunchtime. I was the only one in the office, when a gossamer girl waltzed in. "Is Paul here?" she asked, standing in front of my desk. Paul was the Atlantic Records PR guy.

"Nope. He's drinking martinis in his swimming pool in Marin County while I do his work for him."

She hooted, slapped her thigh, and said, "That figures! They call me the San Francisco Dance Lady—Paul knows who I am. I'm looking for a gig. He represents some of the bands I've danced onstage with."

She walked out the door. Two minutes later, she was back, hands on her hips.

"Since you're doing his PR work, do you want to see me dance?"

I was bored sitting in the empty, air-conditioned office. And I was curious about her style. How was she going to dance without music? "Sure! I'm a dancer, too. Sort of. I don't perform."

Renée flipped her hair back and raised her alabaster arms. She was an angel lifted upward, a heron taking flight, one of Rodin's sculptures come to life. She collapsed dramatically on the rug, then rose like Icarus. She darted about as fast as a hummingbird. She was the size of a hummingbird. This was the best entertainment I'd seen in months and I'd been to a zillion concerts for my job managing backstage passes. I racked my brain. There was something familiar about her and her unique dancing style, but I couldn't place what it was.

She leapt like a tiger, responding to some inner inspiration. When she stopped and bowed, I took her contact info to give to Paul. He took *looooong* lunches, but I was stoked to promote her. Those bands needed some choreographic spice onstage.

Leaving work later that day, walking through the courtyard at the Cannery, I heard sobbing.

There, in a lake of tears, shoulders heaving, hair fanned out around her like limp seaweed, was the San Francisco Dance Lady, collapsed in a pile on the cold concrete.

Tourists passed by as if she were a ghost.

I rushed over. "What's wrong?"

She looked up imploringly, an empty tip basket at her feet, and said, "No one likes my dancing. No one is watching me." Her voice was saturated in despair.

# The San Francisco Dance Lady

"I like your dancing." I crouched down and placed my hand on her birdlike wrist. She was so tragic, it broke my heart. A street artist in the throes of rejection. Just two hours ago, she'd been expressive and assertive as she danced in the high-ceilinged, plush-carpeted offices of the largest record promotion company in the United States. And now she'd morphed into a deflated balloon, a kicked puppy whipped by her own pain.

"You do?" Renée looked up from the hard pavement with wet-lashed child eyes, searching for approval.

It was chilly and she shivered in her sleeveless white chiffon dress and bare feet. I placed my sweater over her shoulders and lifted her off the sidewalk.

Still whimpering, she leaned against me.

"Where do you live?" I asked, not quite knowing what to do with her. She was attached to my arm like a barnacle.

"The cable car men know. Come with me."

Holding a steaming cup of coffee at the cable car turnaround, the burly conductor looked concerned. "Hey Renée! You look terrible. Going home?" He motioned us onto the trolley and waved away my attempt to pay the fare.

As we barreled downhill on Washington Street, the gripman clanged the bell, pulled the brake lever up hard, and came to a screeching stop at the corner of Mason Street.

"Here ya go, Princess." He bowed and helped her down the steps. He nodded at me and said, "You take good care of this little dancing lady, okay?"

She led me to the doorway of what looked like an abandoned storefront. The windows exhibited a sad display of scraggly cactus draped in dusty spider webs.

The door was unlocked and opened into a large room with barely any furniture, a tiny kitchen, and a loft. The pungent vapors of medicinal Chinese herbs and roots swirled in the dim light seeping through the dingy windows. All of Chinatown smelled like this.

I made her chamomile tea.

We chatted for a while about the bands she'd danced with and where she'd gone on tour. Just as I was about to ask why she lived in Chinatown, Renée blurted out, "Do you want to live with me? If you dance, it's free."

It seemed she had just anointed me her new best friend. She was not concerned that I might not dance at all. In her worldview everyone would, could, and should dance.

As I processed this left-field offer, staring into her sea glass eyes, a memory arose. I'd seen her when I was in high school, onstage with the Grateful Dead in Golden Gate Park, dancing in a white Grecian goddess dress. Her long, blonde hair flying like a matador's cape around her head. Backbending until her palms touched the ground behind her. Spinning like a Dervish. A blur of movement. An ecstatic. That's why she'd seemed familiar this morning! I think she had been wearing that same white dress—or maybe she had a closet-full?

I moved in that evening, enticed by the free rent and the surreal environment of living with this bohemian dancer in Chinatown.

When I wasn't working my 9-to-5, we'd wander the city or go to dance gigs. Whatever I did with Renée involved dance. Anywhere. Anytime. She egged me on to join her in the strangest places: supermarket aisles, in the frigid waves at Ocean Beach, on our apartment house roof under the gaze of the Fairmont Hotel that towered over our building. We'd dance nude—much to the delight of businessmen leering from their suites, mouths agape. We didn't care. They were encased in a high-rise and if Renée felt the urge to dance naked, well, she did.

Out in public, Renée always wore those white Grecian dresses—rarely a coat or shoes, even on the foggiest of freezing August days.

In the complete abandon of dancing her way across San Francisco, she would swing from exuberant joy to wretched agony in a heartbeat. I lifted her off sidewalks and bathroom floors more than once. This threw me—even-keeled and normal—off at first. I'd never been around anyone who suffered from eating disorders and overt mental illness.

All I could do was hug her tight until "happy Renée" returned. I was entranced by her magical dance world, but as our friendship deepened and trust grew, I got more glimpses into her damaged psyche. It was a crash course in what happens to many abused children: they grow up to abuse themselves.

She was in love with a teenage prostitute, a runaway like herself. He was effeminate—a beautiful boy—and she was completely taken with him. Perhaps it was their street bond. He ignored her, yet she pined for him. Rejection brought out the worst: the bulimia, the depression. I don't know where she got the energy to dance, but it was her lifeline. For me dance was bliss that filled my spirit and body. For Renée it was resurrection, lifting her out of the misery of her mind and the scars of her body.

I was raised with love and nourishment. My mother's refrigerator was always full and we ate well—everything home-cooked. I was hugged a lot. This nurturing lifestyle flavored who I became. While Mom shelled peas and cored apples, as juicy legs of lamb and sprigs of rosemary roasted in the oven, peppering the rooms in salivating aromas, I sewed. I wrote. I danced. I read. Hemingway's *A Moveable Feast* turned my compass toward Paris.

I'm pretty sure Renée did not eat home-cooked meals. All of her teeth had rotted from malnutrition and bulimia. She'd had them extracted in Amsterdam when she was there on tour with the Grateful Dead. She spent a lot of time avoiding her mother, who had beat her with a hot iron. Renée had the scars to prove it. At 15 she ran away, into the arms of Haight-Ashbury and the Summer of Love. I left home at 18 and moved to Paris. But I wasn't running away from my family—I was running toward a Technicolor life.

Renée's compass arm had been bent, broken, perhaps literally. She danced her way through the perils of street life and found she could live in the spaces between the music and create a way to hold fast and reinvent herself.

I admired her. But I couldn't tolerate her neediness and temper tantrums. Her self-absorption. Her freaky friends. The dancing held us together, though, in a creatively dynamic relationship.

The heaviness of Renée's mood swings permeated the Chinese-storefront-turned-dance-studio. The crunchy, nibbling noises of her late-night foraging kept me awake. After living there for three months and a lot of scarf-waving for Tony and his friends, I was getting tired of them and their hookah pipe haze. I had saved all the money I needed for my trip, and looked forward to flying away from all these crazy-eyed people and commencing my South American adventure: climbing volcanoes, canoeing down the Amazon to Carnival in Brazil, prancing to pan pipes in the Andes. For I knew wherever I went, I would dance—samba at sunrise in Machu Picchu, polka with peasants in the hull of a cattle boat in Patagonia, waltz in a priest's home in the bone-dry Atacama Desert. Dance is a universal language, and Renée had launched my desire to experience life through improvisational movement.

As I left to take the bus to the airport for my Aero Condor flight to Colombia on a crisp September morning, Renée ran into the street and called my name.

"Wait, I have a present for you."

The small package lay in her palm, wrapped in newspaper. Inside was a full denture set clamped around a bouquet of silk rosebuds.

"I made you a corsage pin from my teeth so you will never forget me!" Renée said. "I have a new, whiter pair coming soon from the Haight-Ashbury Free Clinic. I really wanted to give you something special."

I stared at the bizarre gift and then looked down at her. Renée's face was sunken below the cheekbones and her lips rounded over her gums. She broke into a huge, toothless smile, and said, "You really like it—don't you?"

Stunned, I nodded my head, and stuttered, "It is fabulous…"

Just when the Golden Gate transit bus pulled to a stop, she pinned the corsage to my coat lapel. I wondered how I would explain my accessory to the immigration officials. "Wear your heart on your sleeve" had morphed into "Wear your friend's teeth on your lapel."

The real gift Renée bequeathed me was the empowerment to dance wherever and whenever, with music or without. Over the years, I have passed this passion on to my dance students, my family, and my friends. To total strangers who just need the example and permission to cut loose and cut a rug.

Renée is still imprinted on my heart—dancing at Ocean Beach, her hair arcing in the same swoops and curves as the breaking waves. Vulnerable and powerful, transparent and weighty. I'm forever grateful that the magic of the San Francisco Dance Lady has rubbed off on me.

And I despise Rice Krispies.

Somehow, Renée survived her bulimic phase and many other hellacious chapters to get to where she is now, 45 years later: a mom, a wife, a teacher, a cat lover. A rather normal person.

Tony Serra is also alive. A father and grandfather—and still a rebel.

The denture corsage survived as well and occupies a special place in my memento box.

# THE GARDEN OF EDEN

San Francisco 1974

"Did your grandmother give you that?" Delisa asks as we drive into the city through the fog veil enveloping the towers of the Golden Gate Bridge. She's staring at the antique opera glasses hanging on a gold chain around my neck.

Keeping my eyes on the narrow lanes barely visible through the mist I say, "No, Miguel did. He was a gay Mexican man I lived with in San Francisco in 1974. It was his grandmother's."

"It looks pretty fancy," she says. "Is it abalone shell with pure gold frames? Why did he give it to you?"

"He had a mad crush on me—maybe he was bi? He also gave me his grandmother's silver calla lily pin. He came from an aristocratic family in the colonial city of Guanajuato…a gorgeous man, and very sweet." I chuckle to myself.

Delisa asks, "Why are you laughing?"

"Because I was so naïve and dumb back then! Wait till I tell you the Miguel story."

I had just returned from working and traveling in Europe and the Middle East for two years and needed a place to live. I answered a room rental ad on the Clement Street Safeway community bulletin board, which led me to a sun-filled bedroom in a Victorian. Eight gay men were my roommates. (This was before I knew what gay was.) Miguel was one of them.

I had a part-time job delivering organic sandwiches for a company called Moveable Feast. I wore an embroidered peasant blouse and a long, flower print skirt. I made $20 a day, which was enough to live on but I needed more for my next adventure—a trip to the Amazon.

There was an audition ad in the *San Francisco Chronicle* for a dance gig called "The Love Act" that would be performing at The Garden of Eden club on Broadway in about a month. Since I'd grown up in the Summer of Love, I imagined they wanted a hippie dance like in the musical *Hair*. I had been free-form dancing in Golden Gate Park to bands like Jefferson Starship and the Grateful Dead since my teen years, and was confident I could conjure up a dance deserving of the promised $50 performance fee. I just needed to find a partner.

Living with gay men—once I knew what that meant—in a communal household in 1970s San Francisco was a blast. We went dancing every evening at The Stud on Folsom Street. I had eight good-looking dance partners who didn't hit on me, could really rock the floor, stayed up all night, *and* were great cooks. Heaven for a twenty-year-old suburban girl!

At dinner one night I asked who might want to split the $50 a night and be my dance partner. Miguel was game—we did dance together well during our nightly dance-a-thons on the bar top at The Stud.

Every afternoon we worked on our choreography in the living room to "Black Magic Woman" by Santana. Leopard print costumes, diaphanous scarves, feathered headpieces, and tiger stripes drawn on our faces completed our exotic look. It needed to be sexy but we didn't want it to be pornographic. Our theme was Tarzan-meets-Jane driven by a hot Latin rhythm, and the risqué finale was Miguel ripping off my top—just a scarf wound around my bodice. Our plan was that I would flee backstage with him in hot pursuit.

Our roommates thought we'd gone loony as we crawled around the carpeted living room floor in cat-like moves and spun into each other's arms. Doubled over in peals of laughter, Miguel chased me around the couch and down the hallway with my breasts exposed, our startled roommates leaping out of the way. Our chasing evolved into capturing. He would wrap his arms around me, embracing and sniffing and clawing and growling. He had the smoothest skin of anybody I had ever touched—velvet-brown and so appealing. The temperature rose. To my surprise, we became lovers, which magnified our push-me-pull-me attraction.

After a month of this cavorting, we pulled it all into a five-minute routine (without the bedroom hoopla). Our housemates were our trial audience, with one of our roommates serving as the designated deejay and emcee. He ushered everyone into the living room and, with a sweeping hand gesture, invited them to sit on paisley cushions and hushed their chattering. He put Santana's *Abraxas* album on the record player. As a Latin guitar riff swelled from the speakers, Miguel and I burst from behind the hallway door and energetically gave that dance all we had. We scampered from the room, and our audience yelled and clapped.

"Bravo!" "Take it off!" they teased. (I think they were much more interested in Miguel tossing his loincloth into the audience than seeing me topless.)

They all agreed we were absolutely ready for the audition at the Garden of Eden, and I nervously called the club and made an appointment with Vinnie, the manager, for the next afternoon.

Miguel and I took the #30 Geary bus downtown and walked over the chewing-gum-strewn sidewalk through Chinatown and along Broadway to the club in North Beach. Our scant costumes peeked out from under our coats.

We knew we had arrived when we saw the club's two-story neon sign. It showed a giant snake wound around a busty nude woman with flickering red nipples. Eve was holding an apple and looking directly at us. Her eyes were crossed, which choked us with laughter and alleviated our performance anxiety.

Heaving open the studded, burgundy-red vinyl door, we squinted into a dark corridor. Stale beer and cigarette fumes assaulted our senses.

The place seemed deserted. We felt our way down the unlit hallway to a room behind the stage. A pale, red-haired woman in tight cutoffs was filing her nails at a Formica-topped table and noticed us standing there.

"Hi, I'm Candy. You here for 'The Love Act'?" she drawled, popping and smacking her gum.

We both nodded our heads slowly.

"Okay, I'll let Vinnie know you're here. Pick a song out of the jukebox and I'll start it up when you're ready to go onstage."

## The Garden of Eden

Candy seemed very friendly. Holding up the Santana album I said, "We don't need a jukebox song. We brought our own music."

She swiveled her head toward us and smiled sadly at our naïveté. "Sorry, no record player. Gotta pick one from the jukebox. In fact, I'll pick it for you. I've danced to all of them. What type of music do you want?"

I felt like a child asking for an ice cream cone. In a squeaky voice I said, "A Latin theme, please. Our dance is choreographed to 'Black Magic Woman.'"

"Choreographed, huh? I'll try. Get ready. How about I drop the coin in and get the song rolling in a few minutes?"

Miguel and I quickly applied our makeup and headdresses—I was dressed like a hippie-Fred-Flintstone-era Vegas showgirl. Miguel dusted his body with glitter and adjusted the loincloth. His beautiful, sculpted chest and muscular thighs glistened. We climbed up onto the splintery plywood stage. It was small. Not much room for bounding, cat-like movements, let alone all the chasing. We put our coats to the side, avoiding too much contact with the sticky floor, and gave each other a wink and a hug. Then, with our backs to the audience—whom we couldn't discern—we crouched into position as the spotlights blazed on suddenly, harsh light flooding down on us.

At the same time, a country-western number blared out from the jukebox. Was that Tammy Wynette singing "Stand By Your Man"? The song my mom listened to when she cooked dinner? Was I really going to do a striptease to my mom's favorite song—a honky-tonk tune that had driven me nuts as a teenager?

I gritted my teeth. Furrows of confusion clouded Miguel's otherwise perfect face, but we stuck to our routine. We spun around, leapt forward into the glaring lights in our skimpy costumes, and began our dance, peeking through imaginary flora at each other. Me shy and flirtatious; Miguel all sexy-manly. The dance hunt had begun.

I tried to ignore the twangy voice singing the rather un-feminist lyrics to a completely different beat than our movements.

Then I looked out into the shadows of the club. It was nearly empty. A short man perched on a stool, gnawing on a sputtering stogie. Vinnie, perhaps? He was slowly nodding and leering. Another disheveled, greasy-haired man in sagging pants stood next to him, leaning against a broom. His crooked smile revealed gaps where his teeth should have been. I caught the glint of light reflected in liquid on his chin. He was drooling and staring at me bug-eyed.

*What a creep!* kept running through my head, masking the lyrics to the maudlin song. The noxious odors, the goony guys, the gooey floor, the horrid lights were all making me queasy.

Miguel seemed immune to the environment and kept dancing, letting out deep-throated growls and trying to paw me. He reached for my top to rip it off and reveal a brief glance of nubile titty—my cue to exit behind the curtain—but there was no curtain. I panicked, dropped my sex-kitten veneer, and ran down the dirty hallway. Hefting the red vinyl door open, I tumbled onto the sidewalk and into the fog-paled sunlight. In my revealing costume. Barefoot.

I could still hear Tammy crooning through the crack in the door.

*"Sometimes it's hard to be a woman. Giving all your love
to just one man.
You'll have bad times. And he'll have good times, doin'
things that you don't understand.
But if you love him you'll forgive him..."*

I don't think so, Tammy. I'm outta here.

Still shoeless, I bolted across four lanes of traffic on Broadway and plopped myself down at a café table on the sidewalk in front of Ernesto's. I couldn't stop laughing at my stupid idea. Hadn't my mom taught me not to dance in strip clubs? "The Love Act"? What was I thinking? I'll tell you what—$50 to dance. It didn't occur to me that the place would be sleazy. I was absolutely clueless!

Across the street I could see Miguel craning his neck around the Garden of Eden door, looking for me. Eve and her snake flashed above him, her neon nipples glowing in the gloom. Tears of hysterical laughter were pouring down my face as I slapped my thighs. Miguel heard me all the way across the street. Shaking his head, he struggled into his jacket, pants draped over his arm, loincloth still in place, and dodged the traffic. He ran over and asked, "What got into you?"

In gasps I said, "That paunchy, toothless janitor was drooling."

He handed me my shoes and coat as I went on. "I realized if we got the part, we would be up on that rickety stage in a haze of cigarette smoke, and that bloated, horny businessmen would be staring at us with lecherous eyes. They would be drooling, too. Yuck!"

Miguel agreed it was disgusting and ordered us Irish coffees. The waiter was obviously intrigued by our meager, askew attire and face paint, though he didn't ask any questions when he brought the drinks. After all, the Garden of Eden was just one of a dozen strip clubs in North Beach, and Finoccio's—the famous drag queen revue club—was right next door.

The rich coffee spiked with whiskey and topped with a lavish portion of real whipped cream took the edge off. Brushing glitter off his exposed thighs, Miguel giggled and said, "Perhaps we overestimated the quality of artistic effort the manager at the Garden of Eden was expecting. The jukebox music selection should have been a clue."

"What about the giant blinking nipples on that sign?" I said, pointing to luminous Eve across the street. Ordering another round of drinks, I told the circumspect waiter, "With an extra mountainous portion of whipped cream, please. Dancing gives me an appetite."

# HOW I GOT KICKED OUT OF THE PECAN PIE CLUB

Denmark 1972 & Oklahoma 1973

One time dancing really got me into trouble—with a sweet-tempered pecan pie baker from Oklahoma.

Bill was busking on the street in Copenhagen along with other itinerant musicians and performers, collecting spare change for their wanderings. I'd met Bill while traveling. We were both 18-year-old Americans backpacking around Europe. He played a twelve-string guitar and sang original folk tunes, and sounded and looked a lot like John Sebastian, with wire-rim granny glasses and sideburns and everything. He could also do spot-on renditions of Cat Stevens's "Moonshadow" and "Peace Train." My favorites.

I always put a few extra *krone* in Bill's hat when he played Cat Stevens. "Thank you, ma'am," he'd say in a buttery, drawn-out drawl that gave away his Southern roots.

I passed him daily on my way to and from the macrobiotic cafe where I'd fill up on brown rice and tofu. It was 1972, and I was a waif-thin vegetarian who listened to the Moody Blues; Crosby, Stills, Nash and Young; and Joni Mitchell. A true representative of my generation—a hippie budget-traveler from San Francisco, with long blond hair, raggedy-hem denim jeans, and a gypsy blouse, dancing her way around the world.

One day after my coins clinked in his cap, Bill asked, "Wanna get a wheatgrass juice?"

We became friends. He'd walk me back to where we were both staying in the commune city of Freetown Christiania—a self-proclaimed autonomous neighborhood of transients and residents that covered 84 acres in the borough of Christianshavn. Today, 45 years later, Christiania is the fourth largest tourist attraction in Copenhagen—but back then is was an unruly haven for young people where drugs were sold openly. Not the safest place for me to stay, but it was free.

Bill was a real gentleman, escorting me on the dark night streets through sketchy neighborhoods, with nary a demand for a kiss or a hug. I was not interested in getting involved; it seemed like a distraction from my obsession with vagabonding. We'd roll out our sleeping bags in any empty corner of one of the vast abandoned military barracks in Christiania and say *Godnot* (goodnight) to each other.

The northern chill was pervasive and nudged me out of the comforts of Scandinavia. After a few weeks in Copenhagen, I hitched south toward the ripe peaches and sunny beaches of

Greece. Bill headed back to Oklahoma and the University of Tulsa. Denmark was his "gap year" before starting college. We stayed in touch—he'd write to me care of American Express in whatever country I was traveling through, and I'd send him postcards.

A year and a half later, with less than $100 in my tattered pockets, I returned to the States, enamored with the prospect of going to South America after reading the novel *Green Mansions*. I traveled from New York to California on Greyhound buses, stopping to visit friends and family, including Bill on his family's farm in Oklahoma.

I debarked first in St. Louis to visit my dad's brother and his family, whom I'd only met once before. This turned out to be my introduction to the Bible Belt lifestyle.

For the entire visit, my aunt carried a laundry basket through the hallways of their Early American house singing, "Jesus Loves Me." She sang this hymn all day long—out of tune. And she did a lot of laundry. Sometimes, I think she was just washing the same pile of clothes over and over again. The lyrics to "Jesus Loves Me" were burned into my memory, because it was a permanent soundtrack bouncing around the house as she avoided her family. Just her, the laundry basket, and Jesus.

My uncle lived in the basement. He was a bitter man who had beat his kids when they were younger (I saw him do it when they were visiting us in California). He was stronger then, and not yet beaten down himself. Now he was a sad, old WWII veteran who sat in a rocking chair—and he told me all about it. Seemed I was the only one he wanted to talk to. He told me about landing on the shores of Normandy. About surveying the railroad in Indian country. About his epiphany in an Arizona outhouse, the door flung open wide to appreciate the sunrise, that God might exist despite the horrors my uncle had witnessed in the war. He was a good storyteller and the only member of the family who acknowledged I was even there visiting. One cousin, 14 years old, stayed in his room listening to loud rock and dropping acid. My older cousin's wife was staying with them while her husband was fighting in Vietnam. She was a maudlin drunk who hummed the Jesus song under her breath.

Two days was enough in that wretched household, so I got back on the Greyhound bus, rode past miles of hemp fields across Missouri, and got off in Tulsa, Oklahoma, to visit Bill—the musician I'd met in Copenhagen. He lived in Bixby with his parents, on a pecan farm in the farmhouse his great-grandpa had built.

My favorite food is pecan pie. Imagine being at the source! I was as excited about that as I was about visiting Bill. He'd bragged in his letters that his mom was the all-time champion of the Tulsa State Fair pie contest. No one made a more delicious pecan pie than his mother. *Oh boy!* I thought. *Who needs vegetables when you can gorge on pecan pie?*

Bill was waiting in a fancy new pickup truck at the bus station. His beard and sideburns were shorn. He looked almost collegiate. His eyes grew all twinkly when he saw me step off the bus, and in greeting, he lifted me off the ground and twirled me around. His enthusiastic welcome was a bit overwhelming but I figured he was glad to see a person from the wild and free past when he, too, was wandering abroad without a care.

We drove south out of Tulsa through rolling green hills that shifted to flanks of nut tree groves farther than the eye could see. Orchards carpeted every valley and hillside. I was in the heart of pecan country with a pecan farmer's son. And he was belting out the lyrics to "Moonshadow." It sounded as good as when I first heard him sing it on the street in Copenhagen.

The driveway to his family's farm wound through the orchard and circled in front of a perfect two-story white farmhouse with a wraparound porch and rocking chairs. Grand, big-branched oak trees graced the surrounding emerald-green lawn.

A small woman in an apron stood on the porch, waving, as we drove up. Bill's father stood beside her with his arm around her waist and a friendly grin. He sashayed down the wide wooden steps, gallantly opened the truck door, and bowed. "Welcome, Miss California. Hope you are hungry!"

The woman stayed where she was, hands on her hips. "This is my mom," Bill introduced us as I walked up the steps. She scanned me up and down, smiled, then patted my arm. "Come in, dear. I understand you like pecan pie," she said. Her voice was soft and sweet.

As we passed through the kitchen, Mom pointed out three perfect pies crowding the stovetop. I was already drooling. So were the two huge, slobbering hound dogs under the kitchen table; they were staring at the stove, on which a large ham was resting and ready to eat.

Bill stayed in the kitchen to help his mom set the table while Dad gave me a tour of the house and filled me in on who-was-who in the old photos lining the hallway. "This is my great-grandfather. He built this house from scratch and planted the orchards. He had a knack for finding fertile land and a way with nut trees."

We sat down at the solid oak dining table laden with baked ham, chicken-fried steak, mashed potatoes, yams, okra, and green beans. *Where am I going to put that pie?* was all I could think.

Before we dug into the feast, Dad clasped his hands and bent his head. Bill and Mom followed his lead. I copied mechanically, as I was not accustomed to saying grace at the dinner table. Dad cleared his throat. "Dear Lord in Heaven, bless this food. In Jesus' name. Amen."

The prayer activated the tune that my aunt's incessant singing had placed in my head and I giggled. Mom and Dad lifted their pious heads and looked disapprovingly at me. Bill stepped in and said a bit too loudly, "Let's eat!"

My vegetarianism flew out the window as I dug into crispy fried chicken piled onto fluffy mashed potatoes dripping with butter. I held back on second helpings in anticipation of the pie. After we cleared the dinner dishes, Mom placed a pie in front of herself and ceremoniously lifted a silver pie knife while Dad chimed in, "That was my great-grandmother's. It traveled here by wagon train."

Mom poised the blade over the center of the pie and made the first cut. Then she raised it again and lowered it for a perfect 90-degree slice. It slid onto the flat side of the serving knife and she gently placed the slice on a plate with dainty flowers painted around the rim and grandly set it in front of me. They sat staring in silence, waiting for me to take the first bite. The pecans were crunchy, the Karo syrup center oozed like warm caramel, and the flaky crust was layered with butter. A deep sigh of satisfaction escaped me and I clapped my hands and applauded the pie maker. She *was* the master of all pecan pie bakers; Bill had not exaggerated.

All ceremony was dropped as Mom carved up the rest of that pie and dished it out, but a reverent air of quiet devotion ruled as we consumed two pieces each. The second pie was soon just a few crumbs scattered on the bottom of the pie plate.

Bill's family was very welcoming and included me in all their activities. This was comforting after the freeze-out I'd experienced at my uncle's home in Missouri, and I settled into the feeling of being part of a family. Days were filled with riding the tractor, weeding the garden, playing cards, and cooking meals. Mom used a rolling pin that had belonged to her grandma to show me how to make perfect, buttery piecrusts. She also enlisted me in making pecan stuffing for the wild turkeys Bill and his father hunted on their property.

After five days on the farm, Bill took me across the state line to the Ozark Mountain Folk Festival in Eureka Springs, Arkansas, for the weekend. Mom packed a half-dozen pies for our trip, which is about all we ate, as we were too busy two-stepping to the quick-fingerpicking banjo music of Earl Scruggs, grinding our hips to Big Mama Thornton, and swinging it with the Nitty Gritty Dirt Band, to make time for consuming anything else. Bill was less serious than he'd been at the farm and played his guitar around the campfires at night. I hadn't seen it in the house and secretly wondered where he kept it.

As we drove back to Bixby at sunset on Sunday afternoon, exhausted and starving, huge smiles plastered our dirt-streaked faces. Bill said, "That was one heckuva party. I sure miss playing music. Mom and Dad hate rock and folk. They call it dirty hippie music."

Bill turned the truck onto the long gravel driveway, drove past the sprawling orchards and regal oaks, and pulled up to the front of the house. There was Mom in her apron, on the porch, just like when I'd arrived more than a week ago.

But this time her face wore a mighty frown. She looked like she'd swallowed a lemon, and anger flashed in her eyes. This was far from the warm welcome I'd received when I first arrived. Dad was not standing beside her.

"Huh?" is all Bill said as he parked the truck.

Mom didn't budge from the top of the steps. She slowly raised her arm and pointed. At me. Loudly, she said, "She is not to step foot on our property!"

"Huh?" Bill repeated.

"She's a slut! Get her stuff out of your room and leave. NOW!" Mom had escalated her tone to a shout.

*What?*

Her face was now a boiling red. Eyes bulging, she sputtered, "Devil bitch."

*Wasn't expecting that from the Bible-toting farmer's wife!*

I glanced at Bill. Mystified by the hatred so unexpectedly spewed at me, and a little bit scared, I rolled up the window and locked the door, even though it was a humid 95 degrees in the shade. *Is she off her rocker? Possessed by the devil?* I wondered. I knew Bill's family attended some kind of Baptist church in Bixby and that Bill's Dad was a deacon. Had she been overcome with angry spirits? And why was she pointing at me?

She waggled her finger again and through the closed windows I could hear her yell, "Get her out of here! She danced with a black man."

Whoa! That was a twist. What was she talking about? I hadn't seen any black people at the music festival. And Bill's mom wasn't even there. Besides, why would it matter?

## How I Got Kicked Out of the Pecan Pie Club

Bill nervously fiddled with the door handle. Finally, he opened it and stepped reluctantly out onto the driveway. He didn't say a thing, completely ignoring me. He was shrinking right in front of me—melting in his mother's wrath.

Dad was still absent from the tirade, but as Bill went, tail between his legs, up the walk toward the house, presumably to gather my things, I saw lace curtain moving in an upstairs window. Dad was hiding out.

I stayed in the truck, still trying to figure out what she was so upset about. *Did I not eat enough pie? Why would the devil care about that?* A nervous giggle escaped me. Luckily, the window was rolled up so Mom couldn't hear it.

Bill goose-stepped up the stairs and ducked around her, avoiding any contact with the gun-like finger and blazing gaze. She was keeping me in her sights.

Minutes later, Bill edged around her again, holding my backpack. He asked, "Mom, what is going on?"

She shrieked, "She danced with a black man! You come back here but leave her somewhere else—out of my sight!"

We drove north in silence. I pulled the Greyhound schedule out of my purse and found a bus leaving for Los Angeles in a few hours. Bill muttered under his breath, "What the heck?" and I slumped against the door, still wondering what I had done. Off in the distance a twisting, steel-gray, dust-filled devil spun toward us as we raced away from the farmlands. The towering tornado chased us across the wheat fields to Tulsa.

Not looking in Bill's direction, focusing on the impending storm, I said in a flat tone, "I have no idea what is wrong with your mother. Obviously, my welcome has worn out. It's time for me to head home to California."

Bill grunted and nodded his head. He seemed embarrassed and befuddled and unwilling to talk about what had happened back at the farm.

When we reached the bus station an hour later, I stood awkwardly beside him, my backpack at my feet, while Bill called the farm from a payphone. Luckily, his dad answered. Bill answered questions in a mumble, presumably matching his father's similarly hushed tone.

*Is everyone in that family terrified of the possessed pecan pie baker?* I wondered.

Dad continued, "Your mom read Lisa's diaries and found out Lisa had danced with a black man in Switzerland." There was a long pause before Dad added, "She touched him! Lisa touched a negro." I could hear the horror in his voice.

After Bill hung up, I looked at him in shock. "That woman went through my pack and read my diaries? She has no right to do that!"

Bill shuffled his feet on the pavement and didn't say anything. A tired Greyhound bus heading north to Wichita rolled by, spewing exhaust in our faces, adding an even grayer shade to Bill's suddenly pallid skin.

In disbelief, I said, "My mother would never do that. It's private property. She respects my privacy. Your mom is a controlling lunatic—prejudiced, too. And how does she know I even touched him while we were dancing? What an assumptive witch!"

He looked up and said, "She's just bored and trying to protect me."

It was my turn to say, *"Huh?"* Now I was furious. "This woman isn't even ashamed that she snooped and read all my diaries filled with details of two years traveling and working around Europe—in eight journals. She must be *really* bored! And what, exactly, is she protecting you from?"

I stormed inside the Greyhound bus station and bought my ticket to San Francisco via Los Angeles. It was a long ride home away from those crazy Jesus followers, back to my liberal, atheist parents.

Several hours later, as the bus headed out of Oklahoma and crossed into Texas, I scanned my diaries, looking for the incriminating material that had condemned me (in Bill's mother's eyes) for dancing with a person of color. Finally, I found it: "Tonight, I went to a student lounge with Renard and danced with a friend of his from Senegal, in West Africa. I'd never danced with a black man before. He was tall and a very good dancer."

Those were the three controversial sentences Bill's mother had dug out of my journal—the unacceptable truth about me that had shaken her foundation and gotten me thrown out of the pecan pie club. So innocent and yet so incendiary. I had never experienced racial hatred before, and it was a slap of cold-water reality that made me ashamed to be an American.

I returned to San Francisco and worked for a year, saving money for the Amazon adventure. Bill would call periodically and talk about how much pressure he was under to take over the family farm, marry a nice Oklahoma girl from a God-fearing family, and have babies. But he wanted to be a songwriter.

On our last call before I flew to South America, Bill admitted he was engaged to the Bixby High prom queen and had joined the National Farmers Union just like his dad. I imagined him in that little church in Bixby on a Sunday, sitting beside his mom and dad on the same wooden pew his granddaddy had sat on.

I hope the vein of prejudice running through Bill's family has not passed on to his children. Maybe his kids—or grandkids—will find that old guitar in the attic and ask him to play a song. I can still hear Bill sitting on the sidewalk in Copenhagen singing "Peace Train."

*Oh I've been smiling lately, dreaming about the world as one And I believe it could be, some day it's going to come...*

# OLÉ IN PARIS

Paris 1972

Barefoot and shivering in the dark, I shoved the oak dresser in front of the door. Why was I rearranging furniture in the middle of the night? It was all the fault of flamenco.

My date from earlier that evening was on the other side of the flimsy door—apparently incited by our wild experience at the flamenco cabaret. Fists pounding. Demanding entry.

Maybe he was remembering the way the dancers hoisted me onto the tabletop, how my quick-dry flower-print skirt lifted and swirled as the gypsy guitarists sizzled.

I was a student from California who only spoke English and had just arrived in Paris a few weeks earlier, on my 18th birthday. No one danced on tabletops where I came from. I had never even seen a flamenco dancer before tonight. Clearly I had been possessed.

While renting a room at the Alliance Française boarding house (I had promised my parents I would stay somewhere respectable), I met a doctor from Spain also lodging there.

He asked me out on a date. The bland cabbage soup served every meal and tedious daily French lessons taught by mothball-scented, pince-nez-clad instructors were getting stale. Music, dinner, a club! So what if he was half my height, twice my age, had a giant head, and wore owlish spectacles?

The other girls at the boarding house were envious when I showed up in the dining room wearing my fox fur coat and heels.

One of them cooed, "Oooh, going on a hot date?"

"*Adieu*," I said to them in my newfound French vocabulary, followed by *"Tout à l'heure"*—see ya later. They scowled. Then the doctor entered the room and took my arm. The girls burst into laughter when they saw who was taking me out on the town.

The doctor was a gentleman and ignored their rude tittering. He opened the door with a little bow, and frigid December air rushed past as we stepped onto the wet cobblestone sidewalk. He spoke only a smidgen of English, but *no problemo*: I was intrigued by his Andalusian accent.

We walked together, exchanging awkward pleasantries for a few blocks before turning into a passage. It led to a shadowy stairwell that stopped at a splintered wooden door. My date knocked twice, sharply. The door creaked open, revealing a vibrant, smoke-hazed club packed with handsomely striking, dark-haired people. I was the only blonde.

A group waved us over. He introduced me, though it was impossible to gather up everyone's names. Spanish words were layering around me like lace on a mantilla, and enthusiastic *olé!*'s rippled from the crowd to the flurry of dancers among the tables. Fiery guitar strumming and staccato clapping throbbed. This felt like the heart of flamenco in Paris.

The doctor's friends crammed even more tightly together around the banquette, making room. Goblets of blood-red sangria were slapped down in front of us, and impassioned howls and whoops swirled about like a cyclone.

Vibrating on a chair next to me was a woman enveloped in the rhythmic pulse crescendoing on the guitarists' flying fingers. She rose slowly and strode into the space between the tables.

"*Olé!*" the musicians called, then stopped their thrumming and drumming. The other dancers retreated to perch on empty laps and arms of chairs, the rustling of skirts the only sound in this suddenly quiet cavern. With long fingers, she gathered up the hem of her frilly dress that dragged behind her like a bridal gown. Deliberately, she rotated and met our eyes with a challenge.

"Watch this!" her alluring smile commanded.

A black heel struck the ground.

The dancer raised her arms, hands and fingers undulating like hibiscus flowers opening in hot sunlight. Her neck stretched upward, swan-like, head held high. She snapped her fingers and stomped, keeping time with the raking strings and raspy growls of the Spanish guitar that had seemingly fallen under her spell. Candle sconces bathed the ancient limestone walls in amber light, the flames jumping and dipping with the music.

Men in tight, shiny slacks rose from their seats. Women surged forward. They jostled and joined the rousing spectacle. Everyone in the club, from teenagers to grandparents, was a fabulous dancer. I, on the other hand, was feeling intensely out of my element and was not about to add my frugging moves to the mayhem.

Bittersweet sangria flowed freely. Pressed into my side on the cigarette-burned leather bench, the doctor smiled giddily and shouted, *"Olé!"* His sticky hand gently clasped mine. I barely noticed. Then, as if spring-loaded, he shook my hand free and launched himself into the fray. The dancers moved to the sidelines, making way for him in his tattered suit, gleaming black patent leather shoes, and over-large spectacles.

Transformation had never happened so quickly. Lifting up on his toes, arms extended skyward, the doctor was suspended in stillness, smooth and smoky-eyed as Clark Gable. Snakelike, he turned and stared piercingly into my eyes. His tongue flicked across his lips and he lifted an eyebrow.

No one breathed.

He snapped his fingers, accelerating the pace until his hips began to sway. Shouts of encouragement from the crowd propelled him and his feet caught fire, pounding their way around the wooden floor.

The woman next to me unfurled her tortoise shell fan trimmed with lace.

"Él es caliente," she breathed, eyeing the doctor. He was definitely a big fish in this pond.

Damp with sweat, I wished I had a fan, too. It was as hot as Hades. Sipping sangria and gnawing on the tart Valencia orange slices floating in the glass cooled me down. As I set the drink on the table, arms shoved me into the mêlée. The doctor grabbed me around the waist and fixed me with his gaze until I had no choice. I raised my arms and looked downward past his bushy eyebrows into his flushed face.

I clapped and shouted my first *Olé!*

*Really, did I just do that?*

It sounded awkward, like the infant French I was still stumbling over, but after a few more times, it felt right. *"Olé!"* I twisted my knee-length skirt back and forth, mimicking the other female dancers swirling around me. The fabric flew like rose petals in a windstorm.

*"Olé! Olé! Olé!"* My shouts grew louder and louder. With each utterance I felt wilder, stronger—a roaring lioness!

Every table was crowned with a fiery woman spinning and stomping. The dancers were like woodpeckers, making dents in the already pockmarked oak surface with their sturdy heels as, bull-like, the men pawed and snorted around the tables.

Someone grabbed my thighs and lifted me onto a tabletop, and the doctor reluctantly loosened his grip on my waist.

"Ouch!" I shrieked, my skin pinched and squeezed between the fingers of whoever was hoisting me. The *Ouch!* turned into an *Olé!* as his or her grip loosened and I was set free. More triumphant *Olé!'s* followed as I realized I'd graduated to a tabletop stage.

Had someone dropped me into a flamenco musical? Was the sangria spiked with a hallucinogenic substance? These insanely passionate theatrics went on for hours. I didn't have one conversation all night due to the din and the dervish-like fever around me.

Clap, dance, snap, *Olé!*

Clap, dance, snap, *Olé!*

Clap, dance, snap, drink, *Olé!*

What a tornado of festivity!

Finally, the pace slowed down. Clapping ceased. Guitar cases clicked shut. Skirts were adjusted. Shoelaces were tied.

The excitement faded, and everyone clustered in subdued cliques, gulping the ice in the bottom of their glasses.

Ankles swollen, feet sore, I wiggled my toes stuffed tight into heels. The doctor, whom I had almost forgotten about, stood in front of me, ushering me into my coat and to the exit. The wooden door swung open to let us out into the frosty evening, and when we stepped into the winter cold, beads of sweat chilled my skin. I pulled the fur collar around my ears.

On our walk back through the quiet streets, I complimented the doctor on his flamenco finesse and abundant exuberance.

With a gracious *buenos noches* and a dry-lipped kiss on the hand, he disappeared down the hallway. I was relieved he had departed without a request to enter my room. It had been a dreamy evening, but he was not my Romeo.

Pooped, I lay down on the saggy twin bed and wondered why I'd had the misfortune to be raised in a boring American middle-class neighborhood. I could have been born into a gypsy flamenco family, where stomping feet and frenzied dancing were encouraged, and shouting, *"Olé!"* was as normal as frying an egg. At least I'd found my way here 18 years later and extricated myself from suburbia. With a smile of satisfaction, I drifted into sleep.

A sharp rap jolted me out of bed. It was 4 a.m. Slurred whispers of an inebriated man slithered under the door. Then, banging and yelling in Spanish. There was no doubt who was on the other side. With a disgusted grunt and a prickly rush of adrenaline, I pushed the oak dresser in front of the door, blocking his entry before he elbowed his way into my room. What a devil!

Drowsily, I leaned against the dresser for an hour. As morning light dawned and the doctor finally stopped his drunken hammering, I heaved the bureau back where it belonged and opened the door. A crack, no more. No doctor—not even a slumped one in the hallway.

I stormed down to the manager's office. "Why didn't anyone come to help me?" I demanded. "Surely you could hear the doctor's tirade from your room. You could probably hear him all the way to Marseille!"

"It is your fault that he behaved that way," the dour matron replied stiffly. "It's not my problem if you are a slut."

Incensed, I slapped a fistful of francs on her desk to pay the bill. No more cabbage soup or shitty French lessons for me! Bag packed, I stormed out and marched all over the Left Bank, looking for cheap lodging.

On streets I'd never walked before, down yet another narrow alley, a crooked hand-painted hotel sign bearing the likeness of a smiling gypsy woman caught my eye.

I opened the door to the hotel. The woman depicted on the sign was sitting behind a desk in the lobby, which more resembled a living room. Dried flowers hung from the ceiling, and bulging sofas, throw rugs, and a gas fire kept the place cozy. The gypsy wore a floor-length ruffled dress with a neckline showing off her décolletage. Her arms were stacked with clanking bangles.

She barely glanced at me until I asked in broken, American-accented French, "Do you have a room?"

Curious, she looked me up and down. I got the impression she didn't like other women very much, but I was just a girl. Her eyes warmed, a slight smile spreading across her exotic face. "And where are you from, *ma chère*?"

"California."

"Ah, I have a brother in Bakersfield. He sells cars. That's what gypsies do in America. In Europe we trade horses; in America we trade cars."

Maybe it was the lack of sleep or the Alice in Wonderland quality to the place, but I had no response.

Her voice was smoky and redolent—spiced with a naughty humor. "My name is Renee. You may call me Madame and I will call you *La Rubia*." She was quite pleased with herself for giving me a nickname before I even had a room. She winked and asked, "Do you know what my name for you means?"

My tired brain tried to recall my last pitiful French lesson. "Ruby?"

"No, it is what we call blonde-haired people in Spanish." She cocked her head to the side and looked me over again with an air of concern. "Do you eat paella? Couscous? I am a very good cook. And you are too thin!" She waggled a finger at me, causing her bracelets to jangle musically.

I was struggling to stand up straight, I was so tired. "Madame Renee, I love to eat but do you have a room for me?"

She pointed up the stairs and said, "Room six, two floors up. Three dollars a night. Bathroom in the hallway, shower on the top floor. No animals."

The winding stairwell was so cramped, I had to squeeze my shoulders together even though, as Madame Renee had pointed out, I was very slim.

Room six, the last of three rooms on the floor, was perfect: windows that faced the alleyway, high enough for light to stream in—yet it was quiet. It had two twin beds and a bidet I washed the dishes in, much to the horror of my future French friends.

It only cost me $1.50 a night because I rented half the room to Elaine, another Alliance Française student, who had secret liaisons there with her very sexy boyfriend, unbeknownst to her Catholic parents in New Jersey. It didn't bother me that they were swinging from the rafters. I'd be out all day on walkabouts, discovering the delights of Paris. When I returned, usually after dallying on one of the bridges, hypnotized by a glorious sunset splashing coppery-apricot hues on the ripples of the Seine, they'd be gone. Elaine still spent nights at the Alliance Française boarding house for her parents' sake. They didn't have a clue that it wasn't the falsely advertised prim educational haven for foreign students learning French.

On the day I found this affordable haven, Madame said, "You do not have to lock your door here, *La Rubia*. I will keep you safe." It was as if she had read my mind and was visualizing that drunken doctor pounding on my door the night before.

No one was going to get away with any funny business while Madame Renee sat guard in the lobby. She had a sharp tongue and an intolerance for nonsense that made her yell frequently, keeping obnoxious men at bay. Luckily, due to the good looks and charm of Elaine's boyfriend, she made an exception for them, turning a blind eye to their trysts upstairs. When I'd return from my daily wanderings, she'd say, "Too bad he is not your boyfriend! Such a handsome man. Funny, because your friend is very *ordinaire* but I think she is good in bed—like a French woman."

Madame swiftly took a liking to me. I was her daughter's age. I'd spend hours on the stool beside her desk, begging for more stories told in her husky voice about her gypsy upbringing in France.

Flicking a match tip with her fingernail on one such day, Madame Renee lit an unfiltered Gauloises cigarette.

"How did you end up in Paris running a hotel?" I asked.

Smoked plumed around her as she laughed hoarsely. "I grew up wild like the ponies we raised in the countryside. My father wanted to marry me off *really* young, but I was independent. I knew I wanted to raise children who would go to University—the first ones in my family. So here I am in the big city. This is my business. All mine. The children have different fathers."

To keep on her good side, I'd babysit her toddler son whenever she had to run errands or go for coffee with a certain man. She'd bat her dark lashes and soften her voice whenever he visited. It was always a pleasant surprise to witness this sweeter version of her. The man appeared every few weeks with a bouquet of flowers that he picked—or "borrowed," as he once explained to me as we waited for Madame to gussy-up —from other people's gardens. The arrangement depended on the season: violets, daffodils, roses, lilacs, sunflowers. They provided the dried flowers hanging from the rafters. Madame Renee kept every bunch. I was taller than her, so I'd stand on the chair and hang the latest offering when it faded.

For six months I lived in this potpourri palace of funk, loving every minute. Tucked into an alley off of Rue Dauphine on the Left Bank, two blocks from Pont Neuf on the Seine, it provided the gypsy lifestyle I'd been fantasizing about ever since walking into the flamenco club with that Jekyll and Hyde doctor. Every room was rented to some starving artist or vagabond traveler like myself—for I had traded in my student cap for that of an extemporaneous explorer.

I considered myself a student of the world and because my parents weren't supporting me, and I was 18 years old, I could liberate myself.

Day after day, Renee shouted and sang boleros in the lobby, and at mealtimes fishy odors of paella and frying onions emanated from her apartment. The other residents included a curly-haired flamenco guitarist who lived in the attic, a pale fortune teller in the room next to mine, and a grizzled Italian cartographer who suffered from malaria deliriums and never left his room. Best of all was the old gypsy who set up a ladder in the alley below my window. He banged a tambourine while his dancing bear wobbled its way to the ladder top and did furry versions of flamenco. The bear would descend and take the money cap in his mouth, nudging spectators for spare change. I'd throw a franc out my window and sometimes it even landed in the hat.

"No animals, Madame Renee?" I asked teasingly one day. The bear was also a resident and lived in the back garden in a makeshift pen.

"Ma chere," she laughed, "that old man is my uncle. The bear is his family."

Then there was Danny, the odd employee of Renee's who delivered breakfast trays holding steaming bowls of *café au lait* and fresh baguettes to our door every morning. A Hungarian gypsy whom Renee had taken under her wing when he was a kid, Danny shaved his head and wore only a loincloth—even in the middle of winter. He was a kleptomaniac, frequently stealing my few belongings. Renee tipped me off that I could retrieve them in the dungeon-like basement where he also slept. In the hours I knew he was out, I'd go down there with a candle to dig around. Sure enough, my scarf or purse would be under a chair or hanging on a hook against the moisture-seeping limestone walls, the money still tucked into the billfold. For he never really "stole" anything—just moved it around.

At night, we penniless residents were our own and only source of entertainment, and the upstairs rooms of the hotel turned into a combo carny show and flamenco club. We practiced our wine-fueled flamenco moves in the fortune teller's room until Renee yelled up the stairwell for us to knock it off, afraid the floor would collapse and send us crashing into the rooms below. Then, we'd go to the room above to visit the morose fado singer from Portugal with bluish streaks under her eyes, who left her door open as an invitation to enter. A candle burned and a bottle of cheap wine was opened, a few dirty glasses passed around. We'd crowd on the floor, waiting to hear the lyrical moans of sadness seeping through her translucent peignoir.

Sometimes Danny would join us, silently squatting against the wall, smoking clove cigarettes that he heisted from the fortune teller. He'd startle us when he'd leap up nimbly and throw himself into a frenzied flamenco dance wearing only his loincloth. I'd yell *Olé!*, but secretly worried he might get too excited and yank his loincloth off like a matador's cape.

Oddly enough, the fortune teller was not a gypsy—or a very good soothsayer—but a runaway from Estonia. But it did not matter. This strange, Fellini-esque place provided me the freedom to dance and yell *Olé!* whenever I felt like it. In the shower. Out the window to the dancing bear. Everybody else shouted—why shouldn't I? It was a world away from the hushed tones and polite conversations I had grown up in.

Forty-five years after my foray into the world that is flamenco and all things gypsy, I still stay with Madame Renee when I'm in Paris. She continues to hold court in her lobby that looks more like a living room. Her proportions are now more pachyderm than gazelle, her long black tresses have turned a dull silver, and her voice is even more gravelly from decades of shouting and smoking. The rooms have been renovated and cost thirty times more. Madame Renee's coterie of bohemian characters are no longer residents. The dancing bear doesn't live in the garden.

But some things never change: the hotel still smells like potpourri and paella, and I still get a rush every time I shout *Olé!*. It reminds me of that night I bellowed my first *Olé!*, stomping like a barefoot grape crusher with head held high, sangria splashing, just a few weeks into my $18^{th}$ year.

Now, so many decades after my first taste of flamenco, I wonder if that club the horny doctor took me to was a dream. Did it really exist? Every time I'm in Paris, I look down passages and dark stairwells, hoping to find it again.

# THE FLYING FRUG

California 1965

It was the hullabaloo era of the Beatles, The Monkees, the Yardbirds, the Lovin' Spoonful, the Animals, the Kinks. The era of screaming girls, crazed over these mop-head pop-rock musicians.

I had all their albums, bought with my weekly allowance. My parents despised this type of music—Frank Sinatra, Harry Belafonte, and Rachmaninoff lined their record shelf. Saturdays my parents routinely went shopping, and I cleaned the house to earn the allowance that bought my vinyl record collection. I'd crank up the music to the highest volume, bust out the vacuum, and Watusi my way through my chores—twisting and shouting my way across the floor, sucking up dust balls and dog hair.

The music infected us all, even at 11 years old in the sixth grade. For some reason, the principal at our school let us play all the rock-and-roll we wanted during lunchtime. I remember almost nothing about this phase in school except how awful the food was that they dished out—especially the greasy, fried fish sticks on Fridays. And I don't remember any of the kids. Preposterously shy, introverted, and dyslexic, I always sat by myself. But there is one day I'll never forget. It may have been inevitable, given my love of dance.

It was a Friday in early April. A bunch of the popular girls—the future-cheerleader-types with shiny hair, polished nails, and cute outfits, all sure of themselves and cliquey—had grabbed brooms and mops from the utility closet and stormed the stage, where they scrambled onto the six-foot-long folding tables, stood with hips jutting out, strumming their air guitars, and shook their long tresses. Spring fever had infected us all. It was the first time I'd wanted to participate in any school activities as, despite my love of dance, I was *not* cheerleader material.

I looked around, getting the itch to move to the music, but feeling self-conscious and awkward.

The physical education teacher was the only adult monitoring the cafeteria and was also the instigator who turned on the sound system and played the records. As hip as we were and not much more mature, she had all the hits and sang and danced on the sidelines.

As the music grabbed my soul, I scuttled to the side of the five-foot stage and climbed up. I was not interested in being a band member playing an imaginary guitar. Instead, I stood on an over-stuffed horsehair chair I'd found behind the curtain and pushed it to the side of the table. I was going to be the go-go girl. The dancer. Just like in my living room with the vacuum, but now I had an audience.

I twisted to The Monkees' "I'm a Believer," did the Shotgun to the Yardbirds' "For Your Love," pranced my way through Chubby Checker's "The Pony," and gave it all to The

Miracles' song, "Come on Do the Jerk." And my favorite, the Swim, which combined the lower body doing the Frug or the Twist, while my arms mimicked swimming and diving. For the grand finale, I'd hold my nose—just like the dancers on Dick Clark's *American Bandstand*—and pretend to be sinking under water. I didn't even need a song to do this dance!

I was warming up. Getting in the groove. Beaming a big smile out to my audience. Happy to be alive and dancing with abandon.

The chair's iron springs were remarkably bouncy and the perfect platform for an enthusiastic version of the Frug to Herman's Hermits' "I'm Henry the Eighth, I Am," which, at the time, was the fastest-selling #1 hit in history.

The Frug involved pumping your arms in front of you up and down with your hands in fists. I added the bounce. The fast-paced song was perfect for the Frug. Made for the Frug. My arms were alternating the up-and-down flailing as I sang along:

*I'm 'Enery the Eighth, I am,*
*'Enery the Eighth I am, I am!*
*I got married to the widow next door,*
*She's been married seven times before.*
*And every one was an 'Enery*
*She wouldn't have a Willie nor a Sam*
*I'm her eighth old man named 'Enery.*
*'Enery the Eighth, I am!*

The other students eating their lunches loved the show—yelling and clapping; cheering and jeering. The girls on the stage twanged and sang boisterously, though out of tune, flipping their long hair back and forth. We were a hit. I *was* the go-go girl and they *were* rock stars.

The PE-teacher-turned-deejay, still dressed in her white volleyball shorts, swayed and crooned along to the music with the same wild look in her eye as we had. The kitchen staff, wearing hairnets and long, stained aprons, scooped potato salad and served Jell-O cubes and cottage cheese, ignoring us. They weren't in charge of discipline. They just wanted to do their job and go home to their own batch of crazy kids.

Every pre-teen in the cafeteria chanted the chorus:

> *I'm 'Enery the Eighth, I am,*
> *'Enery the Eighth I am, I am!*

The chair was becoming more like a trampoline. I jumped higher and higher, pumping my arms and imagining I was on the stage with Herman's Hermits in front of a coliseum of thousands of wild fans, all Frugging along with me. I was flying in slow motion with my eyes closed. Blissed out. Finding my destiny—of being a gravity-free go-go dancer. My raison d'être revealed at age 11 during lunchtime in Sunnyvale, California. Enlightenment strikes in the darndest places!

Behind my eyelids, colored lights exploded into fantastical fireworks. Then it all went dark.

The next thing I remember is slowly opening my eyes. A blurry vision greeted me: dozens of kids forming a tight circle around me as I lay crumpled on the floor. They were pointing at me, laughing, and asked, "Did you do that on purpose?"

I fainted again. This time, searing pain woke me up. Several kids lifted me off the ground, trying to get me to stand. As they held me up they shook with mirth. "You were flying through the air doing the Frug. It was *sooooo* funny!"

They guffawed, doubled over, and jiggled my arm, not holding it still. The music had stopped, and I wondered where

## The Flying Frug

the PE teacher had gone—I pictured her running hysterically in her pleated white shorts to get a nonexistent stretcher. I was going in and out of consciousness, the lyrics to "Henry the Eighth" echoing in my mind.

As the fog in my brain cleared, I started to put the pieces together, both from my own memory and what the other sixth-graders were telling me: I had launched myself from the chair, off the stage, high into the air, and out into the audience, landing on the hardwood floor that served as our basketball court when it wasn't a cafeteria.

I was Icarus falling from the sky in white-hot ashes of agony. Icarus had nothing on me. This was physical agony and embarrassment in heaps.

The kids walked me to the principal's office and he called my mother, who stormed into the office ten minutes later looking peeved, and she took me straight to the emergency room. My right hand hung limp, the wrist bones snapped cleanly in half.

The doctor said I was lucky because it would not need to be set. "What were you doing?" he asked as he applied the plaster cast.

Nauseous and sheet-white, I said, "I was dancing the Frug on a chair."

"Pardon me?" he asked. "What is a Frug?"

My mother rolled her eyes as I explained, "The dance I was doing to 'I'm Henry the Eighth, I am.'" *Duh! This guy is sooo square.*

He nodded and said, "My daughter plays that music all the time. I hate that song."

"So do I," I said, wanting to cry.

That night my dad suggested I do a reenactment of how I broke my arm. He wasn't familiar with the Frug but as I sang the song that had inspired me to sail through the air, Dad, a history professor at Stanford—and also named Henry—commented: "'I'm Henry the Eighth, I Am,' pronounced 'Enery' with a Cockney accent, is a 1910 British music hall song revived by Herman's Hermits."

*My dad knows this stuff? Weird!*

"The well-known chorus," my dad explained, "is about King Henry's wife being married seven times before. I'm not sure which wife he was referring to, as he cut most of their heads off when they were young."

When I returned to school a few days later, everyone wanted to sign my cast and draw pictures on it of me flying through the air. This time when they held my arm and shook with merriment, it didn't hurt—but it was mortifying. My act was being touted as more of a circus stunt than a mod dance, and the principal had cracked down on performances during lunch, forbidding the PE teacher to play pop songs. She was as bummed as we were.

I think that was my favorite (or possibly only) memory from grade school. Oh, except when my drawing of three naked men running in the Olympics—as depicted on an ancient Grecian vase I admired at the de Young Museum—won the county art contest, also when I was in sixth grade. I was a peculiar child.

Decades later, an excruciating bout of carpal tunnel syndrome in my right hand and arm sent me to the doctor. His eyes widened as he viewed the X-ray and said, "Carpal tunnel syndrome, or CTS, occurs when the median nerve, which runs from the forearm into the palm of the hand, becomes pressed or squeezed at the wrist." He scratched his head and added, "I've only heard about this and never seen a case of it before. This condition is very rare!"

"What condition?" I knew he wasn't talking about CTS, which is common among writers, musicians, and athletes.

He was reverently holding and studying my right arm with great interest. "You must have broken your wrist as a child and the impact was so hard it killed the osteoblasts—or growth cells—in your ulna. That's why your hand is crooked at a right angle. One wrist bone is an inch shorter than the other. Can I take a picture of it to show my colleagues?"

"Sure." Nothing like being *that* patient whose unusual condition impresses even experienced doctors.

I confirmed I had broken my wrist in sixth grade.

"How?"

"Doing an airborne version of the Frug to Herman's Hermits."

He grinned and said, "I always preferred doing the Jerk to *The Monkees'* TV theme song."

"I love that dance!" I said.

He looked at me and shook his head. "Just don't do it on the couch."

# DANCING DIAMONDS

California 1963

Her sea green eyes are pointedly focused on me as I sit next to her on the couch. Her dry, cold hand lies over mine, and tightens. I squirm as her platinum wedding band digs into my knucklebones. It hurts.

But she is grinning stiffly at me.

In a measured tone she says, "My dear, I have a gift for you that no one else in the family wants. They are too cheap to insure it so I'm giving it to you, my youngest granddaughter."

My grandmother doesn't give anything without strings attached. Even at ten years old I know this.

My mother and father sit in wingback chairs across the room by the fireplace. They look mystified by this interaction. My grandmother is not a generous person.

"A girl must have this," she says pointedly, as she dramatically reaches behind her back and pulls out an antique black velvet case. My blue eyes become rounder as she inches toward me. Not quite giving it to me, she breathes on me saying, "It was my wedding present from my late husband,

Mr. Forbes McCreery. I was very young when I married him. Now it is yours."

The touch of velvet on my palms is like reindeer antlers on a moonlit night in the Arctic. My imagination is awhirl with images of what could be inside.

The top flips open and there lies a delicate lacy diamond shiny glittery necklace.

"It's Victorian," is all she says.

My parents sit in stunned silence. They have never seen this necklace before.

Speechless, I rise from the couch; the velvet case lays flat on my palms like an offering. I skip toward my bedroom and close the door. I gently open the case again and am mesmerized by the twinkle and wink of Austrian cut diamonds and platinum lacework that sparkle against the black velvet.

I place it around my neck and the cold of the diamonds on my skin is exquisite. Shivers of pleasure run through me as I realize it is mine. A fairytale princess necklace that has come true. Rarely in my vast imaginary world do objects actually materialize.

Words are not enough to show my awe at such a gift. Words are dull stones, nothing compared to the intricate beauty of the necklace.

I know what to do to show my grandma how I feel about this gift.

I wrap several silk scarves my mother lets me play with around my slight frame.

"Mama!" I call from my bedroom. "Please put 'Dolly Dawn' on the record player."

Shuffling and muttering sounds come from the living room and then the sunshine pulse of Caribbean steel drums and honey butter voice of Harry Belafonte heralds my arrival as I snake my way down the dim hallway, entering the living room with a leap and spin. I twirl around the furniture. I shimmy and shake as inspiration grabs me, and one by one I throw the scarves off as I gyrate like a dervish moth in the flame of joy. All that is left on my naked body is the sparkly gorgeous diamond necklace.

Raising my arms up to the heavens in salutation, I turn and bow to my grandma, absolutely convinced I have given her the perfect dance of gratitude.

She sits stiffly upright on the couch, hands tucked lightly under her soft thighs, mouth wide open, gaping like a fish on land. Staring at my exuberant nudity.

She is Victorian, after all.

# DANCE BITES:

These story selections are write-bites focused on dance—some funny and others on the how, where, and why I dance.

# AN INVITATION

A dyslexic dance teacher?
A free-form dance teacher?
Are these oxymorons?
I'm both.

I'm also a mother, a businesswoman, and was, at one time, an unhappily married woman who had danced in secret all her life, mostly by herself, as a means of artistic exploration and discovery. In private studios, living rooms, faraway tavernas under Mediterranean stars, in the holds of cattle boats in stormy seas off the Patagonian coast—I've danced in many strange places. Until the dream, however, I never imagined this passion being a gift to share, never considered teaching dance as a healing art form.

While perusing books at the local thrift shop—a biography jumped out at me: *Maps to Ecstasy: Teachings of an Urban Shaman* by Gabrielle Roth. It led me to the 5Rhythms dance community, where I discovered I was not alone in my passion. There were other dancers who sought freedom in their self-expression. Not imitation of choreographed scenarios, but authentic movement that evolved from within.

*God, Sex and the Body* was one of the many dance workshops I took with Gabrielle in my mid-thirties, much to my husband's distress. It disturbed him that I was finding a visceral voice for my inner feelings. My dyslexia, which had hindered my ability to take dance classes as a child, was suddenly not an issue, as I wasn't following steps. This set me free. I could dance in a room full of others and connect or not…

I had found my dance tribe. To this day, I attend the Sweat-Your-Prayers-style dance events around the globe. It has proliferated, and there are ecstatic dance communities in almost every part of the world I travel through—Hawai'i, Boston, Paris, Amsterdam, Singapore. We have Gabrielle Roth to thank for spreading the word about dancing for dancing's sake.

Over the next several years, I continued my private dance exploration while studying with Gabrielle. Slowly but surely, tensions and constrictions in my body began to break loose as I danced my emotions. The glacial blocks in my psyche shifted and melted; sometimes it was painful internally, other times blissful. Dance allowed me to travel through my emotional landscape without drowning in the fears and intensities I otherwise experienced. I became curious instead of distraught when large waves of emotion and memory took me into deeper waters of my past.

*What does this dance look like, feel like? Where will it take me?* I wondered. The only way to find out was to let it flow through my dancing body. I was captivated. Suddenly, feelings

I had avoided all my life—had been trained to avoid—were now fuel for creative development. The heartbreak of not having more children, the isolation of learning disabilities, the bleakness of a broken marriage. These feelings were forged into shapes made by my body and rose out of the pain into an art form. Beguiling movements crescendoed and formed from the mud and loam of my life.

Not only did I grow physically and emotionally stronger, I had found my church, my place to dance my prayers, inside and out. Issues such as bronchial illness and gallbladder ailments disappeared. Even my dyslexia, which had always gotten me kicked out of ballet classes (instructors thought I was intentionally going in the opposite direction), evaporated, and I was no longer confused by directional patterns.

So I danced and danced for several years and then, one night when I was 37—just divorced and in uncertain angst about where my life was going and how I was going to support myself—I had a dream that was not a dream. It was a message, an invitation. In the dream Gabrielle Roth swirled past me in a garden, dancing in great swoops and turns. She gestured with a long-fingered hand for me to follow her. I danced behind her through the garden. People were everywhere. They parted as we passed, watching us glide by. Gabrielle entered a maze, a green boxwood hedge labyrinth. I danced after her on the gravel path, around and around the spiral, until we reached the center.

Gabrielle stopped and turned to me, inviting me with a smile and those long-fingered hands, to dance on her head. I rose above her and found myself whirling upside down, our crowns touching. She looked up, gave me an encouraging grin, and laughed. She supported my weight on her head as I spun and wove my arms like snakes in the air. I noticed that crowds of people—thousands—were surrounding the labyrinth and as they watched me dance, they clapped and cheered.

I twirled faster and faster, feeling lithe and free. Then, Gabrielle, who had remained stationary as I boogied upside down on her head, raised her arms to me. I slid down into her embrace, and she pulled me close and kissed me on the lips. It was a seal of blessing. It was sanctification and permission to teach. Even in the dream I was surprised that I was meant to teach. Now? A relative newcomer to intuitive dance with no formal training, what would I have to impart?

I started teaching the next day. Since then, I have taught hundreds of classes and workshops around the world.

Among many other things, dance has taught me this: if your teacher blesses you to teach, do so—no matter how scary or how clueless you might feel about what you have to give. You will be guided by the ones who have walked the path before you—seen and unseen.

And believe your dreams!

# TINA TURNER STILL HAS LEGS

Remember when Tina Turner made her comeback in the 1980s when MTV was blowing up the music video scene? She was closing in on 50 years old. Her dress was short short short with beaded fringe, her ebony skin glowed, and her legs were *stupendous*! Damn. She danced as if possessed by the goddess of sexy fire tower moves as she belted out "What's Love Got to Do With It?" from her new album.

Thirty years later, I went to a jazz club in San Francisco. Pete Escovedo and his big band, including his daughter Sheila E, the cymbal-kicking mama from Prince days, blasted out sizzling Latin riffs. Sitting down while Latin music plays is painful. It was impossible to just sit there, tapping toes and drumming fingers on the tabletop. The band waved their hands upward, gesturing to the audience, get off your butts! And we did.

My partner and I kicked our table to the side and sprang to the dance floor despite the lethargy of the crowd. We didn't want to miss a beat and we had the entire dance floor to ourselves.

We spun and salsa-ed and shimmied—oblivious—on our own isolated island of dance joy in the middle of the floor. Endorphins surged as we laughed in between the spins.

The show ended and, sweaty and exhilarated, we wandered with the chattering crowd into the lobby. We got a few claps on the back from approving peeps who'd probably wanted to be on the floor themselves but were self-conscious.

In the swirl of pressing bodies, a woman nudged in front of me. Her spiky copper mane was the first giveaway, then the distinctive creamy mocha skin. I stepped back and looked down. Sure enough, there were those chiseled legs in stylish mile-high heels– the same sculpted legs as the MTV days. Tina Turner was standing right in front of me. She'd been in the audience. I knew she'd gotten an eyeful of me on the dance floor. I was the same age she'd been when I'd watched her strut and stride across the stage in those shimmery tight dresses, belting out her sexy anthems.

So here's the takeaway for today—get up off your butt and dance no matter what your age! It's soul satisfaction on a grand scale. And ya never know who's watching…

# HANDS DANCING FREELY

There is a way to dance where the movement continues beyond the body. I use my hands to expand my range of expression beyond my physical perimeters. Having the movement continue out the fingertips—like invisible threads of expression—brings a core strength and passion that anchors me in the subtle yet strong unity of my dance. Threads of rippling energy snake upward from my gut, into my torso, through my shoulders, and wind their way through the elbow and wrist joints, unfurling through the fingers and out the tips, painting my dance on a canvas of air. The ability to see and feel the movement whoosh and weave from my feet or core and eventually travel out the fingers is engrossing.

Try it! Connect your hands to your solar plexus and see viscous, stretchy threads unifying the two areas. No matter how far you reach and extend from your core with your hands (or feet), you are rooted in yourself.

I recently worked with a student on this focus. Her hands are her last *frontier for free expression*. They look rigid and block-like when she dances, unlike the rest of her body that is fully engaged and visibly enlivened in the dance. I requested that she hyper-focus the dance through her hands and since she is a professional singer, to connect her hands with the vocal vibrations as she sang. Her hands came to life and appeared longer and fine—her fingers fluttering like butterflies instead of clinging like gnarled, disconnected roots. Her hands turned crimson from the circulation and energy release. She confided that they had ached for years and she had always hated their appearance. They manifested her controlled pain.

My message to you: Fly and be fearless as you reach beyond yourself. Experiment beyond your known patterns of motility. You will paint a new territory through your body. It is beautiful.

# DAYLIGHT DANCING

Dancing is generally considered an evening pastime made for bonfires and dance halls, nightclubs and parties. Dancing in the dark is mysterious—inhibitions loosened by low light and exhibition fueled by alcohol. Boundaries are hazier and people are less self-conscious if they can't be seen as easily as in the stark light of early morning.

One of my favorite times to dance is Saturday or Sunday mornings at the local ecstatic dance in Marin County, situated just north of San Francisco over the Golden Gate Bridge.

"The Sweat" (as we regulars call it) is a peppy event attended by 100-200 people weekly. Held in a high school gymnasium with a wooden floor and lots of windows and airflow, the DJ dance guide plays a wide variety of music, from Andean panpipes, to Balkan chorales, to rock and roll and blues, to the occasional disco number. Even some classical music winds its way into the mix.

It takes me awhile to work up the courage to look at the other dancers—that bright morning light adds ten years to most faces. All those lines and crags can be scary, and it's intimidating to see folks in the harsh light of day, waving their arms around in skimpy costumes and pogo-sticking about to fast beats. Even the younger folk (under 30) look a bit shadowy at first. My mind makes horribly critical comments in a running commentary that, in the moment, makes me chuckle internally but will not score me any good karma points. "There goes Jesus" or "Does anybody in this room have any sense of rhythm?" On and on the dialog unravels in my ego mind.

But before I scare you away from sweating your prayers in the morning with a bunch of other dance addicts, let it be known that despite appearances, it is my favorite time to dance! I have more energy afterward and it puts a smile on my face that lasts all day.

I've got lots of energy in the mornings, and, because it is not a club scene, I can stretch and do whatever my body feels like without a partner. We are all just there to dance. With eyes open, with eyes shut. Stretched out on the floor like a crawling crocodile or leaping about like Nureyev.

As the dance takes hold of me, my mind gives up its need to control and isolate me from other humans. If the room isn't too crowded, my creative edge really has a place to play as there are no steps to follow, just the inspiration of the moment. It is my time to explore my dance and feel the music wind through my tendons. And there is nothing better than being soaking wet from dancing before 10 a.m.!

These ecstatic dances (e-dances) have spread like an underground fungus around the globe. I've recently e-danced in Barcelona, San Miguel de Allende, Paris, The Big Island of Hawai'i, Amsterdam, and Portland—they're even in Kansas! Whatever city you're living or traveling in, there is a good chance your tribe is gathering weekly to celebrate the endorphins released by free-form dancing. No drugs, no alcohol—just sweaty, clean fun.

To find the nearest e-dance source, visit www.ecstaticdance.org, www.openfloor.org, or www.daybreaker.com

# KALANI IS MY DANCE HOME

"Everyone is so energetic." My silver-haired, 83-year-old mom is perched on a plastic chair on the edge of the wooden dance floor.

"And so muscular!" She eyeballs a well-tanned, buff young man with tattoos weaving around his tight torso. I swear I hear her add, "Mmmmmm" as her eyes trail his youthful perfection.

"Mom, did you just say 'Yum'?"

She looks up at me and giggles. "I'm really enjoying myself, dear. Go dance. I'll be just fine!" Her eyes glitter as flamboyant, uninhibited dancers flit past her. Most are sheened with sweat, smiles as wide as palm fronds, tropical tangled hair flying.

It is Sunday Funday at Kalani Honua Retreat Center on the Big Island of Hawai'i—an ecstatic dance ritual my family attends weekly. Hundreds of us gather here with our wild and wacky community to sweat our prayers.

There goes my son Galen, wearing a tutu, performing his swooping eagle and leaping dragon moves. He spins about and heads over to Grandma. She beams at him as his sweat beads and drops down on her upturned face. "Wanna dance, Grandma?"

"No, dear. Watching is such a delight. You go dance!" Off Galen flies, lifting a woman onto his shoulders. She rolls gracefully off his back.

Our partners come from the dance floors of our lives. My mom met my father Viennese waltzing during World War II, I met Galen's dad Sufi dancing in Marin County in 1982, Galen met his love interest Morgan here on the Kalani dance floor just this year, and my love for the last decade—Jordan—is my salsa partner who can easily turn a techno chant into a Latin twist.

My mother passed away several years ago, but every week when we rhumba and swirl ecstatically around the dance floor, I can see her sitting in the plastic chair, nodding her approval and appreciation from the sidelines.

Kalani is our launch pad, our medicine, our church, the house of our true spirit—our dance home.

# TRAVEL SHORTS:

These four stories are micro-bites of special experiences and insights I've had on the road. Take a bite!

# FREEDOM FROM THE SHADOWS
## France 1972

I moved to France on the day I turned 18, my shadow folded in my rucksack. Though the Nazis had been vanquished 27 years earlier, I felt their ghosts along the trails as I traversed the moonlit silver beech forests of the Midi-Pyrénées, and wandered through remote stone villages darkened at night. Residents didn't turn lights on—still terrified of drawing attention from the bombers they imagined flying overhead, still startled at the crunch of leather boots heard marching into their homes, tearing them apart, hunting for human quarry. Stars of David, gypsy clans, effeminate men were all prey to the evil of that war.

What had led me onto this blue-green slate trail winding upward through silent villages, gnarled orchards, and abandoned homesteads set beside crystalline streams?

I was following a map drawn on a sheet of lined binder paper torn from a school notebook. Two weeks before, in Paris, I had noticed a gaggle of students in tie-dye and long hair grouped around the entrance to the Olympia Theater. They had to be American! I stopped and asked what was going on. It turned out the Grateful Dead were playing that night and they were waiting for scalper tickets. One guy chatted me up. He was from Colorado and a student at the Sorbonne, like me. We sat on the curb and talked about the music scene in San Francisco. "Do you like to dance? What are you doing for spring break?" he asked.

I had no plans.

"A group of us are meeting at an abandoned farmhouse in the Pyrenees to dance, hike, and hang. It's free. The farm belongs to one of my friends at school."

So now, two weeks later, with his hand-drawn map, a sleeping bag, and backpack, I had taken the train to Perpignan and onward to a smaller town into the heart of the Pyrenees. The hike up the mountain to the farmhouse was long and arduous, and the trail passed through many of those bleak stone villages.

Along the way, I had plenty of time to think about a book I had read a few months ago. Viktor Frankl's *Man's Search for Meaning* had awakened me to the cruel reality of oppression and bigotry in the world. The book chronicles his experiences as a prisoner in Auschwitz during World War II. During his time in the concentration camp Frankl, a therapist, developed a psychotherapeutic method to help people survive devastating situations. It involves identifying a purpose in life to feel positively about, and then immersive imagining that outcome, regardless of surrounding conditions. This curtain of history was never revealed in my high school history classes. That one could heal from the horrors of a living hell was also a revelation.

The spirit of resistance and indignant fury followed me out of the pages of Frankl's book; as a teenager I was on fire, and the call to danger and rescue appealed.

To fight from the shadows—to be a spy for the resistance, derailing human cargo trains snaking their sinful way to the German borders, was my dream. Alas, I was born several decades too late to join the forces fighting the dark cloud of Nazism in Europe.

But my fiery determination was a start. Over time, the passions remained the same, but mellowed into more poetic pursuits. New goals were targeted in my crosshairs. To be bold and beautiful. To be brave and righteous. To defend the weak and vulnerable. To speak French perfectly—my American accent hiding behind French mannerisms so perfectly, I might as well be a spy. To walk silently, for had I not been a tracker in a past life in the Pyrenees, slipping from shadow to shadow in the dark of night on a mission, or leading children and their families to coastal ports to escape? My imagination was on fire—youthful passion trumping reality, fanning the flames of righteous indignation and fantasy.

I learned to breathe silently, falling in love with crumbling, ancient farmhouses and feasting on moldy chèvre and plonk tasting of iron, sometimes shared with other freedom fighters, or savored alone. I leaned against the smooth bark of whispering trees, my shadow imprinted on their trunks.

The X on the map was accurate. I spent a week with the students doing exactly what my host had detailed: cavorting and dancing to music that blared from a cassette player in the barn loft and eating a lot of granola. After a while, I'd heard too many out-of-tune Grateful Dead songs, so I wandered off by myself during the day.

Called to the loneliness and mystery of the mountains, I climbed higher, resting against haystacks, meandering through forests, and sipping icy creek water, as I imagined the resistance fighters had done decades ago. The secrecy of the mountains was still alive, holding the imprint of those who had walked these same trails to safety—many of whom had given up their lives. Afterward, I had the luxury of returning to the barn and my party-animals friends, dancing to the flower child tunes—not peering from behind tree trunks, wondering who was going to shoot at us or what neighbor might turn us in. It was a very different reality in a very different era. And it was a freedom given us by those who had fought in the wars.

# LICKING ICE CREAM IN BOLIVIA
1975

Six children and their parents are lined up in denim overalls. All flaxen-haired, pale-skinned, with ultramarine-blue eyes set into identical round faces. Each child an inch shorter than the sibling standing next to him. Mom, dad, and their flock are crowded beside me in the narrow, air-conditioned ice cream parlor. No one wants to languish outside in the stifling heat to eat ice cream. Mesmerized, I gaze at their reflection in the mirror on the wall behind the counter. All eight of them are licking their vanilla cones in synchronistic upward laps. Very, very slowly.

This family caught my attention earlier when they circled the plaza in a horse-drawn buggy and parked in front of the ice cream shop. Where am I anyway—in South America or the 19th century American heartland?

I know where I am, all right, and I don't want to be here. I'm passing through Santa Cruz to access the river that flows into Brazil and ride the coal-fueled iron horse that runs from the nearby border into Paraguay. I'm still sore and tired after yesterday's jarring bus ride from the spine of the Andes down to this swampy, alligator-infested *pantanal* (marshy bog), followed by a bizarre, serendipitous wild night with an American man I'd just so happened to meet. Dizzying memories of spinning disco balls and high-heeled babes jiving to Earth, Wind & Fire's "Shining Star" still swirled in my mind.

Santa Cruz is a strange outpost in the tropical lowlands of Bolivia. The plaza, like the town, is depressing—ornamented with a few limp palm trees and splintered benches around the perimeter. Hot, dusty, oppressive, this hamlet is peculiar enough without the straw-blonde clones who just pulled up in their antiquated form of transport, but they are in complete juxtaposition to the contingent of businessmen in dark suits and briefcases who I suddenly spot strutting across the plaza.

I'm exhausted and a bit bewildered. So perhaps I'm delusional and simply imagining these suits striding purposefully to god knows where, as this place does not seem like a hub of international commerce.

Pointing out the window, I ask the man scooping the ice cream, "Who are those men sporting expensive sunglasses and Italian leather shoes? Why are they here?"

Even though I'm speaking Spanish, I can't ask him about the strange moon-faced family, as they are listening and I have no idea whether they can understand. They have leaned toward me, heads cocked to the side in unison—like birds sitting on a wire.

Before he can respond, I have another question for him: "How did they even get here?" It had taken me eighteen hours on an overcrowded overnight bus from Cochabamba to reach Santa Cruz, yet there isn't a wrinkle to be found on the Armani suits and—is that a pink silk tie?

*That's it. I must be hallucinating!*

The shop owner leans across the counter, shushes me with a wave of his hand, and whispers, "Those *hombres* are here to buy cocaine. They fly in on private jets from Miami."

"What?!" I yell, startling the ice-cream-lickers. Now I know what was in those little white packets my date had handed the bouncer and maitre d' last night—that's how he had paid for our extravagant night out!

Just as I stumbled off the bus into the afternoon glare yesterday, a good-looking older American man had approached me in front of the post office and, after we chatted for a few minutes, asked me out to dinner. "I haven't met any American women down here," he said in a Texas twang.

Starving—after subsisting on a diet of Brazil nuts, canned tuna, and oranges for the past month, I jumped at the invitation. Showered, with my blonde hair clean and streaming down my back, I met him in the plaza. We walked a few blocks and stopped in front of an unassuming wooden door with a lion-head brass knocker. A man in a tuxedo opened it and ushered us into a plush, blue-light supper club with a dance floor and leather banquettes—not the setting I was expecting! I looked down at my faded jeans and shrugged.

We were treated like royalty. Champagne, dancing till dawn—women decked out in sequined dresses, gold necklaces, and heels. I consumed mounds of carpaccio, shrimp scampi, and tiramisu, as did my escort, yet money never changed hands. Who cared; I needed a good meal. We did converse, barely, between my voracious consumption of three courses, swilling French champagne, and twirling on the dance floor. My companion's favorite dance moves were the funky chicken and the twist, and he quickly became sweaty and pooped, which allowed me to glide away with a handsome Latin man who knew how to rhumba.

After a few numbers, I rejoined my breathless, balding date, who was on his third Scotch on the rocks. In a loud and slightly slurred voice, he bragged that he was in town to do a business deal with the president of Bolivia, who had a villa off in the bush somewhere. It was a weird night, but I felt so nourished and satisfied from the fancy meal and dancing after being cramped in that rattletrap bus that I let him blab on, not really paying attention to his conversation. He was a gentleman, however. When the disco ball slowed down, he sent me off in a taxi to my *pensione* with a wobbly bow, wishing me a good night.

The next morning, I wandered out into the blaring, bleached sunlight and stifling heat with a specific craving: ice cream. Sugary, cold, and creamy.

So now I stand in the air-conditioned ice cream parlor, scratching my head at the revelation of my date last night being a high-class drug dealer, and trying to connect this to the carriage-driving farmers lined up next to me. What exactly is going on in Santa Cruz? I was expecting macaw-feathered, tattooed tribal dudes with blowguns—not Western businessmen with embossed briefcases and coke straws, or American Gothic farmers.

The fans turn slowly, churning the refreshingly frigid air between our bodies as we lick our ice cream cones. There is only one flavor: vanilla. I lap in silent unison with my pale, overall-clad brethren and ponder, *What other freaks inhabit this bizarre nowhere zone?*

The painful brain-freeze effect of the ice cream stirs my somnolence. It dawns on me that Santa Cruz is not only home to inbred Ma and Pa Kettle colonists, but is also some kind of epicenter for cocaine manufacturing.

Dancing under the disco ball in the middle of nowhere was fun the night before, but I'm in over my head—clueless in a potentially dangerous place. That afternoon, I hightail it out of there to the oddly more normal bug-infested jungle and its tangle of rivers.

# THE DANCING BIRDS OF FEZ
## Morocco 2017

It is not until I leave the interior of the Fez medina and drive the perimeter road circling the ancient fortress walls that I observe the large, pterodactyl-like bird skimming by the car and over the olive groves marching up the hillside. To my left, a verdant riverbed below him bristles with waterfowl, who eye the impressive bird with as much awe as I do.

*Qu'est-ce que c'est?"* I ask my guide, pointing up at the sky.

He does not notice the bird. He's avoiding slamming into on overburdened donkey that is oblivious to all the cars whizzing past as it shuffles across the four lanes of traffic.

The bird swoops close to us, at eye-level. He is huge and dirty-white with coal-black wings that spread out two meters. As he gracefully flaps by in slow motion, a hefty catfish wriggles in his gigantic beak.

A stork!" I yell, flailing my hands. The driver is still not paying attention to me as yet another tipsy, tired donkey steps into the traffic. I recognize the bird as a stork because it looks just like the ones depicted on greeting cards carrying a baby dangling in a cloth diaper from their beaks.

Another stork lifts off from pollen heavy cattail crowding the murky stream that runs down the *wadi* (riverbed) next to the road. The sky is filling with storks, and clouds of swallows converge, mingling with the giant, wheeling birds. A hawk hovers—a still point in the dance of the birds—and then, to punctuate the grays of the stork, the tans of the hawk, and silver-blues of swallows' wings glinting in the harsh sunlight, a troupe of pure-white ibis lift off from the reeds and join the circling celebration of birds overhead.

I crane my neck in wonder, amazed that these birds are abundant in Fez, in a modern era when pesticides and herbicides have eliminated many species. I feel the timeless being of these birds. Clouds and carpets of birds. The trill and twitter of birdsong alive and well.

"*Alhamdulillah!*" I exclaim. As I utter this eloquent Arabic word that means "praise be to God," my driver looks up at the circling birds and, smiling, says, "*Allah ho Akbar*"—God is great.

I learned a new dance move in Morocco that follows me onto the dance floor whenever I'm possessed by the feeling of freedom, of lifting off to cultures so far from my nest. This gratitude has a shape: my arms rise slowly and stretch into the flying stork with wings outspread, circling with my flock in the thermals of a timeless sky.

# WHAT TRAVEL HAS TAUGHT ME

At a literary event I was asked, "What's the biggest lesson you've learned from traveling?"

The answers came as songs from my heart:

We are very fortunate to travel freely as women in this day and age. I also feel this is my first lifetime as a free woman.

The world is an inherently good place filled with kind and generous people who open their hearts, minds, and lives to wandering strangers.

The poorest people are many times the most generous.

To cook for people on the road and share food. In South America, I always traveled in with a wicker basket filled with a tiny portable stove, beans, popcorn, tuna, rice, and oil. I served up meals to starving explorers and Chilean fisherfolk, and heard great stories and drank a lot of wine, sitting on the ground or on porches. For they had experiences I will never have but can live through the teller's tale.

Dance spontaneously with people. I've danced in strangers' homes, on moonlit beaches, and in carnival frenzies in wicked streets. It's a fabulous way to meet people and you don't need to speak their language—dance is universal.

To keep my eyes open so I do not miss the green flash at sunset.

# EPILOGUES

# THE BEAUTY OF LOSING OUR FEAR

> *In many shamanic societies, if you come to a medicine person complaining of being disheartened, depressed, or fearful, they would ask you one of three questions: When did you stop dancing? When did you stop singing? When did you stop being enchanted by stories?*
> Gabrielle Roth

Fear keeps us from expressing ourselves. It keeps us from moving forward—traveling to the Amazon or taking a salsa class or telling a story around a bonfire.

When I was a very young child, I lay under the blankets at night, sheets pulled up to my eyeballs, terrified to reach under my bed and turn on the electric blanket's thermostat. Even as my teeth chattered from the winter chill, I was absolutely convinced that there was a hand—a strong, greedy, pale hand with string-bean-thin fingers and opaque nails—that would grab me and pull me under the bed.

Why did I not place the blanket thermostat on the windowsill within reach instead of suffering? Because my little child mind was frozen with fear. I had allowed an iceberg of intimidation from an overactive imagination to rule my world. What was I so afraid of? Who were the real monsters in my life that crept into my vulnerable sleep world? Who was under the bed? Fairytales, dark movies, midnight visitors?

*And the day came when the risk to remain tight in a bud was more painful than the risk it took to blossom.*
Anaïs Nin

When do we give a voice to our unfounded fears? Or to our real dreads, boiled up from past memory?

Even beauty scares me sometimes. Still, as an adult. It is not the shadow in the alley or the autocrat with a nuclear button. It might be a beautiful man, absolutely terrifying in his gorgeousness. A monster ready to destroy me with his magnetic appeal.

Funny, huh? Afraid of beauty.

Even my own beauty. As a younger woman, I hardly ever looked at myself in the mirror.

This is not so true anymore. Now I find beauty in the dark and in the light. And in the mirror. The grabbing hands I imagined as a child have faded away. I'm able to appreciate all shades of reaction, attraction, and perception. I'm especially entranced by the weak and silly parts of myself. The best stories are hidden under the bed!

The most beautiful of the beautiful are the particles of vastness that shimmer behind the eyes, under the tree bark, dancing on the dangerous curves of the sea. But you have to be brave and look to see the shimmer.

# ELEVATE US FROM THE SHADOWS
## prayer and poem

*There is no shadow to dance with at night
under the dark of a new moon.
Untethered to the spongy grass and
red cinder path, my movements unrecorded.
Not daguerreotyped onto the expectant ground.
Not even a whisper of a shadow plays within
the fluid movements of my dance.
Invisible choreography woven from dreams and desires.*

*On this dark night, I dance in dialog with a spell,
wanting to weave the world whole again.
Light and dark elevated
beyond suffering, stupidity, fear, greed.*

*Elbows lift, arms outstretch, fingers reach, torso twists, eyes call to
the sapphire purity beyond the darkness.
Beauty and goodness revive.*

*Dancing in pure shadow—with no witness.*

*Please.
Elevate us.*

—Lisa Alpine, Big Island of Hawai'i, 2019

# ABOUT THE AUTHOR:

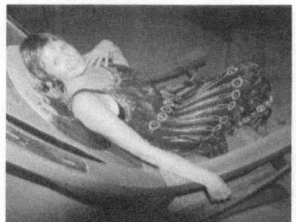

Author in her favorite chair—Havana, Cuba

Lisa Alpine is a well-known dance teacher, travel writer, and author. When not wrestling with words, exploring the ecstatic realms of dance, swimming with sea creatures, or waiting for a flight, Lisa divides her time between Mill Valley, California and the Big Island of Hawai'i, where Pele's lava dances at the edges of her writing retreat.

You may buy her other books — *Wild Life: Travel Adventures of a Worldly Woman* (Foreword Reviews' Gold Medal Book of the Year Award) and *Exotic Life: Travel Tales of an Adventurous Woman* (1st place North American Book Awards) in every format on Amazon and all other literary outlets around the globe.

Her award-winning, dynamically delicious stories grace the pages of many anthologies, including Travelers' Tales *Best Travel Writing*.

Read her monthly online magazine about travel, dance, writing, culture, and inspiration at www.LisaAlpine.com

# DANCER, HEAL THYSELF
## Marin Independent Journal
## By Christa Bigue

Teacher, writer, world traveler - Lisa Alpine wears many hats. But it's really her role as dancer that provides the Mill Valley artist the most satisfaction.

"Dancing is No. 1 for me. I gear all my other passions around dance because dance gives me the greatest joy and expression. It's my art form," said Alpine, who's taught dance as a healing art form for decades.

Her approach, known as Dance Weaver, combines storytelling, poetry, travel, sculpture, nature and dance into classes and workshops around the world and in her Mill Valley home studio.

"I guide students into deeper, stronger and more expressive ways to dance, which will enhance existing dance patterns and develop new skills and techniques," Alpine said. "I hope students come away from any of my workshops with a sense of empowerment, confidence, familiarity and curiosity about their own artistic exploration and enthusiasm to continue their development," she said.

Indeed, Alpine is known for her intuitive ability by opening up people through dance to their expressive nature. She wants her students to "wake up to new movement" and "develop the ability to unlock energy pathways and direct vitality to where your body needs attention," she said.

The mainly self-taught artist has studied with Gabrielle Roth, Emilie Conrad and other master teachers/shamans but, there is no method to her free-form dance teaching. Alpine draws inspiration from African and Latin dance teachers and designs her workshops around "my curiosity, passion and experience," she said.

"There is no end to the learning curve for myself or my students. I'm always weaving new themes and artistic aspects into workshops, so there is a constant sense of discovery."

Students range from all ages and nationalities, but they do share one common trait: They want to explore their creativity through dancing.

Many of Alpine's students are writers, grappling with a creative block, self-consciousness or a "stiffness of the mind and body," said Alpine. "I show them how the two art forms benefit each other, how the dancing loosens the words and stimulates verbal descriptions and expressions to let the writing flow."

Other students include people recovering from a physical injury or wanting to "integrate the left and right sides of the body and brain in movement, which increases balance and acceptance of who we are," Alpine said.

Professional ballroom dancers also come to Alpine to "open up the flow a little bit more so they don't' look so trained," she said. "They may be technically perfect, but ease, grace and flow means letting go and not controlling the movement so much."

Rita Glassman of Sausalito, a cantor at a San Francisco synagogue, describes Alpine's workshops as supportive, empowering and inspirational.

"She's a highly intuitive teacher, who knows how to draw out the muse and the best in each person." Glassman said. "Working with Lisa, I have come to recognize that to dance or to write with awareness and the willingness to take a risk can often lead to a more fulfilling life, as well as a greater connectedness to oneself and others."

It's through dance that Alpine healed herself from dyslexia, bronchial illness and gallbladder ailments, as well as an unhappy marriage.

"Dance allowed me to travel through my emotional landscape without drowning in the fears and intensities," Alpine said. "Suddenly the feelings I had avoided all my life were now fodder and fuel for creative development."

As people found out what she was doing in the studio on her own, they asked if they could study with her.

Alpine's love for dance began when she was a young girl, "secretly dancing wherever I could," said Alpine, including living rooms and private studios and later as an adult throughout her travels in "far away taverns under Mediterranean stars and in holds of cattle boats in stormy seas off the Patagonian coast," she said.

"I've danced in many strange places, but I never imagined having a gift to share."

When her son Galen was born, Alpine took up writing and started *The Fax*, a Marin County community newspaper.

She also started teaching travel writing at The Writing Salon and was the travel columnist for *The Pacific Sun*.

Still, it's dance that everything else in her life revolves around.

"I crave movement and have found dance to be very grounding and healing," she said. "It is truly an expressive art form you create from your core. Dance releases a lot of material and gives expression to the abundance of who we are and who we aspire to become."

# KUDOS

This book had several coaches and midwives. I bow to Laurie McAndish King—author, good friend, and crack editorial consultant. Our weekly meetings assisted both of us in the shared voyage of book writing—helping each other over the hills and through the valleys of muddy story birthing.

After Laurie and I hammered those words into shape, I'd send them on to Amberly Finarelli, who has been the professional editor for all my work. She embodies a huge sense of humor, a spiritual streak, the practicalities of a mom, and a guide to the narrative arc that takes the story to the finish line.

My love interest for the last decade is a Buddhist with a fine brain. Jordan Scott—or "The Great Jordini," as my son and I have titled him, deserves that red satin Superman cape I keep threatening to sew for him. We don't always agree on the exact story message or where each word should go, but he sits on the couch as the sun rises, coffee cup in hand, and listens to my unborn children of the page. Bless him! Or maybe he should bless me because he is the novice monk...

And to my son, Galen Marc Alpine, who has kept me balanced and grounded since his conception on the side of an active volcano in New Zealand.

# FABULOUS POSTS
# FREE MONTHLY EZINE

DANCE STORIES & VIDEOS

TRAVEL TIPS & ADVENTURES

WRITING TOOLS & ESSAYS

HEALTH & INSPIRATION

CULTURE & ART

FOOD AROUND THE GLOBE

SIGN UP AT WWW.LISAALPINE.COM

Merci beaucoup
Gracias
Thank you

These stories find their way into people's lives via
reviews and word-of-mouth.

If you have enjoyed them,
share your enthusiasm and support by
writing a review on Amazon and posting on social media.

Blessings!

Lisa

Foreword Reviews' Gold Medal Book of the Year Award for Travel & NABA's Best Travel Book of the Year

From licking a Monet in Paris, to pushing an abusive macho honey-mooner off his sailboat in the shark-infested Galápagos, to saving her toddler son from a charging bull elephant in Africa, these delightful tales will inspire readers to follow the call of a wild life and leave home with their doors unlocked.

> "Lisa's love of travel and her fierce determination to push all boundaries, takes the reader with her on a thoughtful, fun and fearless journey."
> —Maureen Wheeler, founder Lonely Planet

*Wild Life: Travel Adventures of a Worldly Woman*
(Life Series #2)
Product details: $14.95 print book. $7.99 ebook. 208 pages
Published by Dancing Words Press 2014
ISBN-13: 9780984229369

Available in paperback, ebook, & audio wherever books are sold.

# Winner of the BAIPA Book Award for Best Women's Adventure Memoir

"*Exotic Life* is a sprawling anthology of 19 travel tales. Alpine is an inspiration to women travelers everywhere. She fearlessly wanders through one obscure destination after the other, leaving her complete trust in the experience. She answers that timeless question – Can solo women travelers really go there? – by doing just that and carrying away some wildly unique stories." —*Rolf Potts' Vagabonding*

"Lisa's travels are more than exotic. They are wonderful reading. I have to say this book stayed with me for a long time, and I loved the last three lines about Guadeloupe." —*20th Annual Writer's Digest Annual Self-Published Book Awards review*

*Exotic Life: Travel Tales of an Adventurous Woman*
(Life Series #1)
Product details: $12.95 print book. $6.99 ebook. 196 pages
Published by Dancing Words Press 2010
ISBN-13: 9780984229338

Available in paperback, ebook, and audio wherever books are sold.

www.ingramcontent.com/pod-product-compliance
Lightning Source LLC
Chambersburg PA
CBHW020645300426
44112CB00007B/248